T0206822

AFTER THE HOLOCAUST
THE BELLS STILL RING

AFTER THE HOLOCAUST THE BELLS STILL RING

Joseph A. Polak

Foreword by Elie Wiesel

URIM PUBLICATIONS
Jerusalem • New York

After the Holocaust the Bells Still Ring
by Joseph A. Polak

Copyright © 2015 by Joseph A. Polak

Typeset by Ariel Walden

Printed in Israel. First Edition.
ISBN 978-965-524-162-4

Urim Publications,
P.O. Box 52287, Jerusalem 9152102 Israel

www.UrimPublications.com

In memory of

Table of Contents

Foreword by Elie Wiesel

Distinguished colleague, charismatic teacher, lover of Jewish culture and tradition, Rabbi Joseph Polak sees himself above all as a survivor of Bergen-Belsen. His experiences as a child in occupied Europe affect his thinking as deeply as his loyalty to tradition.

During the several decades we spent together at Boston University, we fell into the practice of devoting several hours everyday delving deeply into a page of Talmud, into the ancient debates between the Sages, teasing out, as well, their meaning for today.

Learned, brilliant, with an insatiable intellectual curiosity, always open-minded, he knows how to pause in the middle of an obscure talmudic passage and there uncover an intellectual or ethical link to contemporary reality.

To study with him was for me more than a passing joy; it was a return to the past. With him to my right, or opposite me, the volume of Talmud open on the table, I once again was my adolescent self in my little village in Transylvania, in *cheder*, chanting the old passages written for us by our ancestors.

We rarely spoke of the war. Sometimes, though, it appeared, springing forth, uninvited, like a question one doesn't expect. How did our Sages find the strength and the means to fight the hate which surrounded them? What is the lesson that becomes our legacy from them? Faced with the questions confronting our generation – that of Auschwitz, naturally – what can we do to be faithful to them? How would they themselves have behaved in Birkenau?

A profound believer and scrupulously observant, he is fully admired and beloved by our students. They appreciate his desire to share his knowledge, his experiences and his intellectual and moral courage to challenge what is prohibited for the benefit of a great discussion. For him, as for me, a good answer does not replace a good question, but confers a new dimension upon it, transforms it into something different, more profound, further inaccessible, but also inexhaustible.

For all these, and for so many other reasons, writing the foreword for his book is far greater than a gesture; it is a confirmation that some encounters remain timeless.

They raise anew the human miracle.

Elie Wiesel
Summer, 2014

(translated from the French by Martha Liptzin Hauptman)

Prologue

Almost *every year since 1991 an annual conference of child survivors of the Holocaust has taken place. Typically, four to five hundred participants are in attendance, forming, among other possibilities, a kind of therapeutic community in which one's history may be reconsidered in a validating setting, where everyone is as afraid as you are of their past, where mourners may mourn their dead and, where necessary, their living, and receive a measure of consolation no other segment of society can offer. For many child survivors, the Gathering, as it is called, has become a pilgrimage, and for those working to organize it, a high point in their personal lives.*

I have attended a few of these Gatherings, and in the fall of 2009 I was asked to address the plenum of this group, whose members had been through the Holocaust as toddlers and children. For this occasion I chose to read selections from this memoir. What follows in this prologue is what I said to them as an introduction to that reading. I can think of no better way to begin my story.

Ladies and Gentlemen:

We are gathered here, the children — *the children* — the last survivors of the Holocaust. We who played around the horrors of Bergen-Belsen, we who were hidden by loving parents who disappeared, often never to return. And if they did return, it was often with shame, with mindlessness, with madness, sometimes incapacitated emotionally and physically.

What could our surviving parents and guardians have been thinking, when, having seen what we saw, having lived in circumstances so depraved, so deprived that there is no historical parallel to them; what could they have had in mind when, at war's end, they placed us in regular schools, in regular camps, among regular children? On what basis did they think we would adapt, somehow – which none of us did?

So many of us did not know how to eat normally, did not know how to play at all. Some of us knew love only from parents who we never saw again, or from adoptive families from whom we were seized after the war.

For many of us, the Holocaust only began after it ended in 1945.

It was only then that we became aware, and started to process what we had been through, what our families, if we had any left, had experienced. The 1950's, the decade of nocturnal screaming, the decade of social silence. The decade of everyone presuming that the Holocaust was behind us, that horror and evil could be put behind us. Two child survivors I know had their parents shot in front of them when they were ten years old, each in different Polish ghettos. How could anyone imagine that these children would *get over it?*

We, the child survivors, were told by our surviving parents if we had any, or by their friends, if they had any – what do you know about the Holocaust? You were just a child.

This invalidation, this negation of all that we had gone through, whether or not we possessed verbal memory at the time, whether or not we could articulate our experiences, was to say to us – you are not who you say you are, you are just a normal kid.

We were not normal kids. We had been too sick – from our isolation, from abandonment, from typhus and dysentery – to be normal kids. To say to us "what do you know, you were just a child" was to tell us we were not who we thought we were, we were not survivors like those grown-ups. We experienced, in this way, the Jewish version of Holocaust denial.

Then, forty years later, there was a maturation. At this time, we found each other. We laughed together, we wept together, we did some extraordinarily delayed growing up together. We opened doors, memories, feelings that we didn't even know we had; we settled scores with parents long gone, with guardians of ours in different times and different places. And we did an awful lot of forgiving.

Some of us learned to speak to God, to ask Him what He had in mind, in the midst of the one and a half million children who were slaughtered, in allowing *us* to survive.

And yet here we are, on this Sunday morning, eating danish and sipping coffee, at once shattered and whole; at once sad and celebrative; wanting to tell the world that the human spirit cannot be extinguished by evil, nor by sadness, nor by horror.

I wanted to say to you, the last survivors, the youngest, that to be asked to speak to you this morning, to read from my memoirs, is one of the greatest privileges of my life.

Blessed Are You, Lord our God, who has brought us to this day.

Introduction

I am a child survivor of the Holocaust, one of the youngest. My Holocaust began just before I was born. I was not yet three when the war ended, and have but a few memories of those dreadful years, some real, some imagined. When later in life friends learned of my imprisonment in Westerbork and Bergen-Belsen, none of them could persuade me to speak about any of this – in part because it was too painful to think about, in part because I had only the vaguest knowledge of what had happened to me in those years, in part because societal forces would not *allow* me to think about those times, and in part because deep, powerful currents in my soul resisted exploring this darkness.

This book is a study of those years, to be sure, but it is especially a study of their aftermath (1945–1953), and of times even later on when events and experiences that I *do* remember transpired. While the Holocaust was not in any articulable way in my memory, it was nonetheless within me. It often surprised me, not to mention those around me, by popping out at the most unexpected moments, making me a witness in search of his own testimony, a witness whose survival defied odds, and whose story, for which he had little responsibility, nonetheless had to be told, again and again.

My tale argues against the popular idea that the Holocaust

ended for its victims with the conclusion of World War II. It is a mirror held up to the immediate post-war years to help understand what had befallen us earlier, when we were taken away. It begins, one might say, where Anne Frank (whom Mother said we knew in Bergen-Belsen) left off.

Beginning with the anti-Jewish measures instituted by the Germans and their local supporters, victims of the Holocaust had the management of their lives progressively and systematically removed. It began with being robbed of their assets and continued with being fired from their jobs. When their livelihoods went, so did their identities. Children in school saw their classes diminishing each day, with the kids who had been mysteriously summoned to the principal's office never returning. What questions posed in the minds of those who remained? What dread?

When, after the war, the few survivors straggled back from the camps or from hiding (some 5,000 children emerged from hiding in the Netherlands alone after the war), they were faced with the disappearance not just of their families and friends, but of their communities, losses in numbers so large that they defied apprehension. Of all the emotional blows the Holocaust dealt its victims, none, it seems to me, was more devastating than this. Although one is not wired to imagine men with earned doctorates tossing live infants into the fire-pits of Auschwitz, it was even more difficult to learn, as did the survivors of the city of The Hague, that of the 35,000 Jews that had lived there before the War, fewer than a thousand shuffled back, damaged and enfeebled, in August, 1945. Neither imagination nor intellect are themselves sufficient to make sense of evil of such magnitude, yet there it was, in all its exponential horror. One was more than shaken by it, one was emotionally incapacitated by it.

I try to show in this book, mostly through the memories of my post-war years, that with respect to the Holocaust, you never "get over it." It is a great and terrible lesson that has nothing to do with psychopathology. You can lead a reasonably healthy and productive life, while constantly feeling that it can happen again, at any moment. In the early 1950's, Mother and I never failed to be terrified whenever the doorbell rang unexpectedly. This ringing of the doorbell and its attendant terror of round-up and death is an image I develop in the first chapter called "Percussion."

The second chapter of the book (entitled "Tanya") is unlike the others in two important respects. First, outside of the talmudic quotes that helped shape it, it is fiction: completely the product of my imagination. Second, it is the only chapter written like a play, rather than as an historical narrative. If it appears, at moments, to be too parochial, I nonetheless respectfully urge the reader to stay with it. It offers its own rewards, and it comes up again at the very end of the book.

The book is also a meditation on this early segment of my childhood, when I moved from playing hide-and-seek amidst the hunger, the dysentery, the typhus, and the 30,000 unburied corpses of Bergen-Belsen, to playing once more a mere eighteen weeks later in the basement of a synagogue in The Hague. There, a pathetic remnant of children, worn and wild, most of whom had only recently emerged from hiding, gathered on what seemed like weary Sundays for religious instruction. As I will relate, many of us who did have a surviving parent, returned reluctantly, often against our will, to a scarred, damaged creature, whose competence for living, much less parenting, had been deeply impaired.

Years afterward, my almost pathological reluctance to examine my Holocaust background changed dramatically when I turned fifty. Suddenly I found myself hurtling backwards into time, still afraid, haunted by poplar trees which still unsettle me, and by the harsh sounds of Dutch which could bring me to nausea.

In some ways, the gathering of material for this memoir became part of the process of unearthing my past. My first attempt to do so as a writer was in an article that was published in *Commentary* in 1995, entitled "The Lost Transport" and which forms a central chapter of this book. The careful reader will discern that the article contains no reference to my Dutch past – with which I was simply unready to deal at the time, and that it contains only a partial description of my reconciliation with Mother. In this book, I reprint this chapter exactly as it appeared in 1995, and in the next chapter, I have added a new section describing the reconciliation more fully to be faithful not just to memory itself, but to record the post-Holocaust battle with the terror of memory that rarely abates.

I added the chapter on Westerbork because few seem to know about this place, and because what went on there illustrates more poignantly than any other Holocaust experience I know how the unraveling of identity, the loss of ego and of one's sense of self, was very much part of the strategy of the educated SS.

I also write about Westerbork because of the poplars. All my life I experienced a disturbing, chilling fear of poplar trees, a fear that I could make no sense of, save that it was associated with that icy gray chill in my bones that I knew to be the Holocaust. I looked for what remained of the poplars in Bergen-Belsen, and they were not there, nor were they in the village of Troebitz. When I finally visited Westerbork in the year 2000, there they were. In a twist of irony, after years of ignoring them, I noticed that Yad Vashem, the Holocaust Museum and Authority in Jerusalem, was surrounded by acres of them. Tall, mighty trees, cruel in their inaccessibility, narrow, armless and green, bespeaking, perhaps only to me, chaos and murder. Life out of control, and most of all – armlessness: no one will reach out to help you, nothing can save you.

The last chapter, entitled "The Last Witness," while not written as a play, picks up where the second chapter ends.

★

The teacher within me says that my book will read more easily if the reader spends a moment understanding the following brief chronology of times and places:

- October 16, 1942: I am born in The Hague, German-occupied Netherlands.
- September 29, 1943: My parents and I arrive at Westerbork, where over a period of about 24 months, more than 100,000 Jews are forcibly gathered to be transported to points east.
- February 1, 1944: Departure with parents from Westerbork to Bergen-Belsen
- April 9, 1945: Departure with parents from Bergen-Belsen on an SS-controlled train with 2500 fellow passengers, to Theresienstadt.
- April 25, 1945: Train is liberated by the Russians in a gentle village called Troebitz, deep in East Germany.
- May 4, 1945: Father dies, and is buried in a mass grave in Troebitz. Mother, health failing significantly, is given up for dead.
- May–June 1945: I travel with other children by train from Leipzig to Holland, and am there adopted by a Dutch-Jewish family.

- July or August 1945: I am reconciled with Mother in her hospital room in Eindhoven, Netherlands.
- 1945–1948: Mother and I share a room at a center for Jewish survivors of the Holocaust in The Hague, Netherlands.
- December 1948: We sail for New York, en route to Montreal.

I write for all the children, who like me, survived because others were prepared to risk their lives for us, and out of gratitude for the miracles which we experienced in those years almost every day. I write also for the one-and-a-half million children who perished unattended by miracles, so that they too not be forgotten.

May the generation following ours be worthy of the prophetic vision that "nation shall no longer raise its sword against nation." May we be worthy of living in a time when people will no longer say that the other, by virtue of his beliefs or practices, real or imagined, has forfeited his right to exist.

JOSEPH POLAK
Winter, 2014

BOOK ONE

CHAPTER ONE

Percussion

This is what she says: "The Nazis came to our house in the middle of the night."

"They came," Mother said, "they came," she accused, "with motorcycles, with guns." "They banged," she said, "they banged with the guns on the door." They pounded incessantly on the door – no let up. The pounding does not subside – they will not go away, they will knock until the end of time, and even after that they will pound into the blackness of the night. The percussion of the Holocaust. Diabolical intrusions, life irrevocably interrupted. You realize that the pounding will never cease, that they will pound until you are dead, or until they are, it is then that you understand not just that your life-trajectory has been irreversibly disturbed, but also that your autonomy has come to an end, your sojourn among the world of choosers is now over. In the evenings, you will no longer draw the curtains, shut the lights, close the doors, and conclude the day. You have tumbled into the latrine in which all choice ends.

Someone opens the door, and police wearing jackboots climb the stairs bearing guns and bearing lists. Were you to think that it is the guns that gave them their authority, you would be wrong. The guns helped set the scene, delivered the sense of terror, but it was the lists, the lists, that gave the Nazis their authority.

The lists, the endless lists, the six million typed names brought to our houses on those black midnight visits – it was the lists themselves that allowed the bearers to pound on our doors until we could no longer take it, the lists that allowed them to pound with the relentlessness of the pursuer. Had there been no lists, they would not have come, would not have pounded. It was the Jews, the Jews, who had, before the war, prepared the lists.

What to make of this. When does order, the possession of lists, the ossification, the finalization of bureaucracy, become formidable enough in its autonomy to establish the paraphernalia of murder? The *Joodse Rad*, the Dutch Jewish Council, in delivering the lists to the Nazis, was not knowingly suicidal. Yet the murder of 102,000 Dutch Jews could not have taken place without the lists, without the bureaucracy, without the typewriters and the foolscap and the carbon paper and the onionskin. It could not have taken place but for the addresses, the birthdates, the professions that the lists provided.

The list is what snared you. It was terser than you, more to the point than you; neater than you; in its own way, more real than you. Your birthday was on it, your address, your occupation. Its authority lay not just in its data but in that it was typewritten. Typewritten meant official, official meant authority, authority meant license. Each name and its accompanying detail occupied a line; the approaching end of the line was signaled by the typewriter bell, and soon after it rang, the next line, with its next victim began, so that the bell tolled for you, and for each person after you. Six million bells rang in those years. Six million bells indicating six million verdicts, indicating six million deaths, six million murders.

My father lies in a mass grave in a churchyard deep in eastern Germany, where the bells still toll. Christians sought him out, Christians murdered him, Christians buried him with Christian love, Christians still tend to his grave sixty years later with Christian love and deep remorse. Christian bells still disturb his great slumber, echoing the bells from the typewriters in the *Joodse Raad*, where he had worked and on which he had no doubt typed. The typewriters which upon printing the names, tolled the doom of the victims into eternity. Shall we, as a memorial to the six million, call for the silence of all the Christian bells of Europe? The percussion, the percussion of the Holocaust. A friend who, like myself, is an infant survivor of the Holocaust, has been the chief percussionist of a major symphony orchestra for over thirty years. What rings for *him* from those bells?

★

I am still not born. After the war, Mother is prepared to repeat the tale as often as I want to hear it (which is pretty much never). When I am finally prepared to hear it – by which I mean to internalize it, to appropriate it – she is long dead, the tale is on tape, and I am bursting. I cannot hold myself back from traveling to The Hague, to find the house, to find the door they pounded on. No mention of anyone ringing the bell that night.

Don't have a clue where in The Hague this house is. Don't know if it survives. Don't know how to find it. It is summer, 2002, and I think (incorrectly, I later discover) that anyone who might remember is long dead.

In Amsterdam, at the War Historical Institute (NIAD) I find, fluttering in the microfiches, the prisoner lists compiled in Westerbork. Oh, the sailing, tumbling names of the microfiches! How they float directionless, not to heaven, not to earth, like ash from a chimney. I scour the ever-trembling plastic, I enter the rain of ascending and descending souls, I duck bodies, avoid faces. Everyone waves, thousands, tens of thousands of them, graveless, this is their final imprint on earth, the typewriter bell tolls at the end of each name; again at the end of each address. We lived at 82 Wetteringenkade, The Hague.

Two stories, part of a row house, a sex shop nearby. There are two buzzers on the doorpost, one for a downstairs apartment, the other for a small duplex townhouse. Perhaps a shadow where once a mezuzah hung. The police came up the stairs, Mother had said. I have found the place, and it does not look as though it has ever seen better times.

Who answered the door that night? Grandmother Rika? Did she put on her *sheitel* for the Nazis? Perhaps they broke the door down. Did her son, my father, answer? Too good natured, too much love for the world – more reality in the pounding than he could altogether bear. Don't know.

They come up the stairs in their jackboots. Mother, nine months pregnant with me, is under the covers.

"What are you doing here?" she accuses – she had a powerful voice which she saved for occasions such as these, or for when, while in high school, I came home much too late at night. On such occasions, in Montreal, sitting invisibly in the pitch dark dining room that abutted my room, she would use this voice, which never failed to frighten me, to ask – "Where have you been?"

I don't know what the Nazis said, something, I'm sure, about our having to leave for Westerbork. It is about 4 a.m., and the dawn has not yet broken through the Dutch sky.

The same voice says to them, "What's the matter with you? I cannot go to Westerbork, I am in my ninth month!" A silence, broken only by the irregular thunder from motorcycle engines outside making the house tremble, finally ends with one of them saying to her, "If this is the case then you will have to show us the pregnancy."

"Nothing, nothing in the whole war," Mother later said, "was more humiliating than that moment. Not even the barracks of Bergen-Belsen." Her laments on this were filled with sobs of horror that drew you into their rhythm: "A Jewish woman," she would repeat again and again and weep as she repeated it, "a Jewish woman. Imagine making a Jewish woman get out of bed to show them."

They left. The motorcycles roared into the distance and as dawn slowly rose over The Hague on that fall morning in 1942, a hush fell over our household. I can't imagine that anyone went back to sleep. I can't imagine what else was done, what else was said.

★

Who was there? Who witnessed this event? Father is eerily absent from every narration. Perhaps Mother was unwilling to remember, relate or judge his helplessness on the occasion. He must simply have stood by: there was no alternative. She spoke of the event as we would today of a rape. In the old Wild West movies, I sometimes think, they would have known what to do. The script would have called for a tobacco chewing grizzler pulling out his Winchester, looking the buzzards squarely in the eye, and saying something like, "Get offa ma land." My mother took on this role, and I, bleating in the exposed swollen belly, I am the one to become protagonist, to have saved the day.

The Holocaust thus begins with an act of incapacitation.

When a parent realizes that he can no longer protect his children, and is thus perpetrating the deepest of all human betrayals, then it is in the shame of this helplessness, like the crack of the neck when the noose fully tightens, that the breaking of the human spirit begins. "They can take away your children," you suddenly realize, "they can take away your children, and there may be nothing you can do about it." An ontological failure has been exposed from which, if you recognize it for what it is, you may never recover, and after which you will be irreversibly mad, incapable of parenting again, should you manage to survive and start over. You will challenge your child's every movement towards independence; you will have to steel yourself not to crush his spirit. Or, you may well turn child-rearing into a spectator sport, with your non-survivor spouse doing the job, as you look on, helplessly, despair-ridden, unskilled, lost and sad; if you're lucky, doing only marginal damage as the child grows up.

I have no visual memory of Father. I think I may have some sense of what his voice sounded like. He succumbed to typhus and malnutrition before I turned three, that is to say, he was murdered by the Germans before I turned three.

What were the consequences of this brief triumph of being saved from immediate shipment to Westerbork? Were there lessons learned? That Nazis (Mother always called them *The Police*) were suckers for hard-nosed encounters, that they were no match for the disposition that came from strong character? Did anyone think that they wouldn't be back? An interlude, to be sure, had been provided.

But what an interlude! When they finally came to get us, a full year had passed. We arrived in Westerbork on the 29th of September, 1943. At least half of my murdered Dutch relatives had already come to their end in the death camp Sobibor, and by

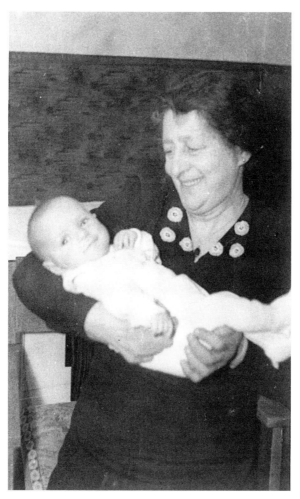

Hendrika Polak, Father's mother, and me, early 1943, before we were all sent to Westerbork. She was subsequently murdered at Sobibor, like everyone there, within three hours of arrival.

this date the Nazis were no longer sending Dutch Jews to death camps. The last train from Westerbork to Sobibor was on July 20, 1943. The reprieve of a year from the Nazis' first visit may well have saved our lives.

Grandmother Rika was not so lucky; she was gassed in Sobibor. Mother never spoke about the circumstances of when they came to get her mother-in-law. She was in her seventies at the time, a religious woman of deep dignity, and certainly where I was concerned, a repository of unlimited love.

★

What did Mother and Father say to each other in the aftermath of this triumph, framed as it was in a double humiliation – Father's powerlessness, and Mother's belly-baring? Father hunted for business during these days, and when he found small jobs, shared them with other families, to bring in, as they said in those days, a little income.

CHAPTER TWO

Tanya

Note: This chapter, the only one of its kind in this memoir, is a fantasy in a talmudic setting. The quotes from the Talmud which trigger the reflections are authentic, and appear in bold-face type. The description of the circumstances of my birth is likewise authentic.

Tanya [an Aramaic word meaning "we have learned"] . . . when the child finally passes [from the womb] into the world, that which was sealed [the lungs] is now opened, and that which was open [the navel] is sealed. Were it not this way, the child could not survive even a single hour [on earth].

SCENE: The heavenly holding tank, from whence souls depart to enter the world, and to which, upon death, they return. It is very crowded. Among the comings and goings, the returnees are in overwhelming majority. A montage of harrowing sounds, one atop the other: We hear automatic weapon fire; dogs snarling and barking furiously; an interminable, unintelligible speech in a bad microphone by the Fuhrer making him sound as though the back of his throat were lined with bubble gum; shouts of "Hear, O Israel," the proclamation pious Jews recite twice daily, and if they can, before they die; children, children, in numbers larger than the mind can accommodate, cowering before some horror, and weeping, and weeping; their consoling moment, the one grownups know to anticipate, disappeared into some invisible future, even in this higher world where all is revealed and all is transparent. And Mozart, of course; lots of Mozart. An angel appears, he seems to be wearing noise-abatement earphones. The date is 16 October, 1942.

ME: Let me out of here! Too much! Too many children, too much crying. Why is it so crowded? Why don't they stop crying?

ANGEL: They *died* crying and screaming and are not able to stop.

ME: Why not?

ANGEL: Perhaps because their trauma was so great, their outrage so beyond any ever experienced, that even their deaths failed to console them.

[*aside*] (Perhaps also because they wish to drive God mad.)

ME: Who are they?

ANGEL: They are one-and-a-half million Jewish children, without sin, about to be or already burnt alive or starved to death, led by hapless parents. *They don't want to enter the gates of Heaven.*

They don't trust entranceways. The camp gates promised them freedom – they don't believe in promises at entranceways, don't like going from one place to another. They're not even interested, it turns out, in the promises offered at *these* hallowed gates.

Think about it. How could they imagine that God would be here for them? Where was He in the world where their little bones now lie cremated in a mountain of ashes seven tons thick in Majdanek, seven tons of madness in which the silence of their screams is overwhelming? So they refuse to enter the gates, they were betrayed at the gates of the earth, and are terrified of a repeat in Heaven. They did nothing, they shout, to deserve the fiery furnace on earth – how could they trust what's in store for them in Heaven?

ME: How will it benefit them if God is mad?

ANGEL: They weep out of outrage: they have experienced a magnitude of injustice, of humiliation, and of physical suffering not imaginable by mortals, perhaps not even by immortals.

Their suffering challenges the very omnipotence of God Himself. Could *He* have thought this up, they ask – could He have *planned* this for them as part of their sojourn in the world? Is this what is meant by the prayer, "He prepares the steps of men?" To presume this is to offend God in the deepest ways, and to contradict all that is said about Him in the Torah.

Yet to claim that He was helpless in the face of the great and murderous slaughter of the children is equally offensive.

They cry because they have arrived in the Hall of Justice and have found it wanting for judge and trial. And so they will cry and stamp and pound their little fists upon the two empty thrones, of Justice and Compassion, until the end of time. And even as the voices of the Torah can never be silenced, neither can their sobs. So coterminous are their voices with the Torah, that it is not always clear whether the crying comes from the martyred children or from the Torah itself.

ME: Are you saying that God has abandoned the Torah?

ANGEL: No, to the contrary, that He has taken refuge in it.[1]

---

1. "Said R. Ilai the son of Berahya: Two scholars living in the same city with dissonant ways in halacha; when the one dies, the other is exiled"

ME: How long will He stay there?

ANGEL: Have you not studied the laws of the blood avenger? If a man, the Torah relates, unintentionally kills someone, then the relative of his victim has the right to destroy the murderer in revenge. But if the unintentional murderer flees to the city of refuge established for him for just such eventualities, he is there offered sanctuary from the blood avenger. I am not suggesting that God is implicated in the murder of the Jewish children – this is beyond anyone's capacity to judge, save for Him alone; I am merely explaining from whence we derive the parameters and limits of sanctuary. To answer your question: He is free to leave the sanctuary after fifty years, at which time the blood avenger has no further claim on him. (Check out your Talmud, Sotah 49a, in the name of R. Ilai ben Berahya).

ME: Then He is overdue?

ANGEL: What is a single year in the eyes of the Lord?

A light is kindled over the head of the child about to depart for the womb. In a sweep that extends from one end of the universe to another, he stares at the world for the first time, contemplating it as one might in a dream [taking it all in, missing nothing].

Indeed there is no hour in the human experience when a person has it as good as when he is still in the womb. Here is he taught the Torah in its entirety . . .

ME: Tell me, then, why am *I* not crying? Am I not myself about to enter that furnace?

ANGEL: Because although you will pass through the fiery furnace,

---

(B. Sotah 49a). Here exile is used in an allegorical way, and from this usage I obtain license to do the same.

you will also survive. You will have seen everything, but you will remember very little.

Yet as soon as the child leaves the womb to enter the world, an angel taps his mouth, causing him to forget all the Torah he has just been taught.

ME: So I will be a witness who, because of the amnesia of childhood, will have forgotten most of what I have seen of the Holocaust, but will still be a witness for having been there and for having been a victim.

ANGEL: You're not hearing me. The children continue to scream for eternities after the Allies win. The Holocaust does not end for its victims in 1945. It is only the war that ends. In fact, the infant survivors, of whom you will be one, who never had family nurturing before the Holocaust, will suffer some of the most debilitating consequences of all the child survivors.

So the trauma, the suffering, the damage to all survivors, continues for generations. You will be a witness to all this, perhaps the youngest, perhaps the last. You will be a prime witness not so much to the Holocaust as to its sequel – those horror-filled years following 1945.

ME: Is being a witness easier than being a martyr?

ANGEL: I'm sorry, I never meant to suggest that. But witnesses have their own sets of problems. They have issues of credibility, and anxiety that what they witnessed will soon be forgotten. So while they may scream, they are more likely to go around tugging at people's sleeves, trying the patience and emotional limits of their listeners, and telling their stories over and over again.

ME: So when my time on earth is up, and I return to the Celestial Court and want to tell my story, will there be Anyone there to hear it? And if there is, won't it be impossible to concentrate – don't you find this crying hopelessly distracting?

ANGEL: The King, whom we entreat on the Day of Judgment to move from the throne of Justice to the throne of Mercy, is no longer very much apparent in the Hall of Judgment, and instead it is the children who sit there, their faces ashen, their hair grey, weeping, weeping, not understanding.

There *they* inquire of every returning soul – what have you done during your sojourn on earth to avenge our slaughter? How have you restored love and compassion and justice to the world? What have you done to shame the perpetrators? The bystanders? To call them and their descendants for ever after to account? Have you asked God about us?

ME: Children are not commonly known for their compassion. Can anything I will have accomplished on earth be adequate for them? Suppose I want to speak to God directly.

ANGEL: You will have to ask for Him by Name.

He has repaired to the Beit Midrash, the Celestial Study Hall. There the meaning of the Torah is plumbed; there He scans the holy text (which, you will recall from Genesis Rabbah, was His blueprint for the world), both in its written and oral forms, for an accounting of Bergen-Belsen and Sobibor and Belzec, so that *He*, at least, may understand what happened.

ME: Is the crying of the children not audible in the Beit Midrash? Are not so many of the Holy Martyrs already there, their fingers drumming on the study tables, bursting with questions and accusations?

ANGEL: The Beit Midrash is where He can *manage* the crying, and where in His Torah, he can find consolation for His slaughtered children. Do we not read in Psalm 119, "Were it not for the balm of Your Torah, I would have long ago perished in my affliction?" Does not the *Torah Temima*, himself scheduled to succumb in the Warsaw Ghetto, teach this in Deuteronomy 4:42?

Perhaps here He can recover enough to once again be the Redeemer of His people, and to effect their consolation, for Israel remains grievously unredeemed and, like the child victims, utterly inconsolable.

ME: I'm not sure you're serious. But do tell me, while He is exiled in the Beit Midrash, who is running the world?

ANGEL: After you have witnessed Bergen-Belsen I suspect you may not want to ask this question.

Yet [the unborn child] does not depart that place until they have administered an oath to him, as it is written, "For unto Me every knee shall bend, every tongue give homage."

"For unto Me every knee shall bend": this is the day of death, as it is written, "All [those] descending into the earth shall kneel before You."

"Every tongue give homage ['oath']" – this refers to the day of birth, as it is written [in the Psalms] "of clean hands and a pure heart, whose soul has neither sworn falsely nor with deceit."

And what is the oath administered to him?

"Be a righteous person, not a wicked one. And even if the whole world tells you that you are righteous, in your own eyes remain wicked."

Know also that the Almighty is pure, that His servants are pure, and that the soul placed within you is pure.

Yours is to preserve your soul in its purity; if you do so, how marvelous; otherwise I shall pluck it out from within you.

ANGEL: It's time for you to start moving towards the departure lounge. Please don't tarry; there are timing issues with your birth.

ME: If God is in exile in the Beit Midrash, who is managing the great Hall of Justice in His absence? Surely not just the children?

ANGEL: You point to a grave problem. There is no justice possible when encountering these children, their voices hoarse, their eyes filled with a pain no mortal can forget, and from which no immortal can be immune. There are no facts that can be established, as in a court of justice, one can only shudder and weep and ask that they sentence you any way they see fit. Usually they are too deep in their suffering to even acknowledge your presence. It's a problem: No one, no one, not even – dare I suggest it? – God Himself can get past the children.

Yet somehow souls do, and had you studied more assiduously, you would have learned that the unintentional murderer we just discussed does not go alone into exile; his yeshiva is required to accompany him. The yeshiva provides plenty of judges to manage the assessments of the lives coming to heaven for judgment. As we learn in Sanhedrin 6a, God, in recusing Himself from adjudication, is in total observance of Jewish law in this regard. But that is not the same as saying that He is not mesmerized by every life brought for review before the Court, and spellbound by every story.

ME: So if we assume, as you imply, that God committed Himself to the observance of Jewish law, then is He not Himself in danger of being judged?[2] Has He not stood by, in some fashion, as His "brother's" blood was spilled? Has he not allowed the most profound idolatry in history to triumph, where He commanded His people precisely to destroy such idolatry?

2. Midrash on "*Maggid Devorov leYaakov*, etc."

ANGEL: There is probably some such danger, but it may be diminished in the yeshiva of refuge.

ME: But – bear with me, I do need to know – can you really replicate the conditions of the great Hall of Justice in a Beit Midrash? If returnees, much less the Judge of all the earth, are judged only by the statutes of the Torah, wouldn't this result in judgments so technical that they would be in danger of being all justice and no mercy?

ANGEL: In the heavenly Beit Midrash, when someone is being judged for evil and no one can be found to exonerate him, I have heard that they call up Rabbi Akiva, who once boasted that if a court were under his jurisdiction, no defendant would ever be sentenced to death. And so they ask him – Akiva, holy Master, tell us how might we defend *this* particular *shlepper*?

Then Rabbi Akiva, the fire of his own martyrdom at the hands of the Romans burning in the black coals of his eyes, rises before the Heavenly tribunal and, as only he can, argues the exoneration of every victim – gassed or burned, starved or drowned, learned or ignorant, pious or free-thinking – and personally escorts him into the Academy on High, where, like the Temple in Jerusalem, there is always room, and which is lit, as nowhere else in Heaven or upon Earth, with the lamp of truth.

ME: Rabbi Akiva must be one exhausted lawyer.

Has he been called in to defend the Almighty?

ANGEL: He has, and has refused. Perhaps because a King is not normally tried in a Jewish court of law, perhaps because he loves Him too much, perhaps for some other reason. He has remained silent on the matter. But little soul, it really is time for you to take the great oath.

ME: No way. I'm not going.

There is no justification that you can provide that will convince me to head into that inferno, that cauldron of madness where every semblance of what God had in mind for the world has disappeared. No one there can observe His commandments, neither during the inferno, nor especially in its aftermath. No one will ever be able to be truly joyous again without every smile betraying the victims of the gas and the crematoria.

To witness, you say? Why do I have to witness a world that God Himself doesn't understand? Why is this my lot? I don't want to be one of those screaming returnees, their mouths open in perpetual horror, their teeth black with the hunger of a thousand wretched fasts. You are asking me to be a player in some kind of curse, and I refuse. If you overpower me and send me down there, I will say that I am not subject to the covenant at Sinai because it is cancelled at the entrance to every death camp.

I am not going into that inferno. You are asking too much of me. I'm not prepared to live with the screaming of the children. I will not have what it takes to abide it, not when I lie down, not when I rise. I feel as though they are screaming at *me* because I represent the unfairness of it all, they are being slaughtered and I survive.

ANGEL: When, out of your mother's womb, you enter a world where of necessity most things are hidden, you will be free to decide whether or not you want to hear their screams. You will be free to forget about the Holocaust and live as though it never happened.

ME: Not to hear them is to betray them. Take those earphones off!

ANGEL: Little soul, we are running out of time. Your mother is in labor. She is driving to the hospital with your father. Your survival will be the result of a series of miracles of which your birth is but the first.

ME: What kind of miracle?

ANGEL: A company of German paratroopers has landed near the hospital your parents are driving to. The soldiers have incurred all kinds of casualties in the jump, and the hospital is full. Their commander has secured the hospital and has ordered the managing physician to concentrate exclusively on his men and refuse admission to any new patients. The company commander and the physician are at the entrance of the hospital as your parents drive up, your mother is visibly progressing in her labor. They are expecting her. The Nazi looks at your mother and tells her that the hospital is full, would she please find some other place to have you. The physician also looks at her, and then calmly speaks to the German: "Sir, if you do not allow us to treat this woman, then my staff and I will refuse to treat your soldiers. You will have to attend to them on your own. Let me also point out, if I may, that if you shoot us for my intransigence, you will still have no one looking after your troops." The German officer shrugs and curses.

And that is how you will be born. Now please recite the oath.

ME: No way.

I've thought it over. I'm not going down into the world precisely because I *am* going to survive. When you claim that God saw *me* fit to survive, then doesn't that mean that He didn't see the one-and-a half million children as fit to survive? Isn't that ludicrous? How could you expect me to live with this?

Yet how could I *not* be grateful to Him for the miracles of my survival? So then how can I not express my appreciation to Him? And when I do, how do you suppose the one-and-a half million child martyrs will feel? What would you like me to say to them when I return to this place and face them?

Forget about it. I'm not going. And yet . . .

ANGEL: What is it?

Me: What's your name?

ANGEL: All you are doing is prolonging your mother's labor. Your descent into the world is not a matter about which you have any choice.

ME: But I do have a choice about the oath, otherwise it wouldn't be an oath.

ANGEL: You are right. Do you find anything objectionable in the oath? If you do, I am happy to talk it through with you.

ME: At my mother's expense, right? You're very slick. I have no problem with the oath itself; I have a problem with the screaming and the weeping.

ANGEL: Please recite the oath.

ME: Only if you tell me your name.

ANGEL: What possible use would you have for my name? I can tell you that I am with Dispatch, that is all. I am allowed to bless you and to promise to be at your side. Isn't this enough? Please – recite the oath.

ME: I will recite the oath if you promise to either tell me your name or give up those noise-abatement earphones. If I must live with the screaming and weeping then I need you to hear it as well.

ANGEL: I will go mad if I hear the children crying unto eternity.

ME: That is how I will know with any certainty that you are at my side, per your promise.

ANGEL: Do I have a choice?

ME. Not if you want me to swear and go.

SCENE: [Angel removes earphones, and soon, slowly, inexorably, softly, starts crying with the children.]

ME: Now then; bless me.

ANGEL: What blessing would you like?

ME: *Bless me that though I will witness so much horror, that I also witness the realization of Isaiah's prophecy: that the "Almighty will wipe the tears off every face," and please especially have the children in mind as you quote Isaiah in your blessing.*

   Bless me that I be the last survivor, and that, therefore, one day my passing mark a great transition: where joy will be fully and legitimately restored to the world, as to the world-to-come.

ANGEL: Why don't you wait and see if joy is possible in the world even though there are still survivors around? What makes you so sure . . .

ME: Do you want me to take the oath? How far is she dilated?

ANGEL: Amen, amen, amen!

CHAPTER THREE

Who's Going on Tuesday? Westerbork

According to the records of the Joodse Raad (Jewish Council), Mother, Father, and I arrived together at Westerbork on the 29th of September, 1943. We were deported to Bergen-Belsen a mere four months later on the 1st of February, 1944. Mother never mentioned Westerbork while I was growing up, and while I had heard of the place, even had forebodings about it, I did not connect it to my own story. In a 1995 journey of remembrance meant to revisit the sites of my early life, a journey I describe in a later chapter, I chose to skip the visit to Westerbork with which the journey began. This was hardly a rational skip; it probably had to do with my incapacity, which persists, to see myself as a Dutch Jew.

Yet sometime after my fiftieth birthday, I decided to explore Westerbork; something, I know not what, gave me license to do so. In the year 2000, a new journey brought me to a reunion there, at the camp site. I found myself among an extraordinary group of people, survivors, to be sure, but also of Dutch men and women who, in those dark days, had hidden Jews, and who shared Westerbork as their symbol of the Holocaust. This chapter charts that visit, and the visit becomes the framework and background for describing the camp.

I

And so it is that I stand here at the maddest spot on earth, among others also gathered to so ponder, to suffer its absurdities. Here, where once stood a camp in which there was little killing and little typhus, little hunger, little thirst. A camp which had a soccer team, a hair salon, and a weekly cabaret, a camp in which, it seemed, only the elderly died.

I stand here in Camp Westerbork, the mouth that sucked you into the vortex of the Holocaust, from which nearly 100,000 Dutch Jews were deported to Auschwitz, Sobibor, Bergen-Belsen, and Theresienstadt, with no notion of where they were going, except that it wasn't good. And when the elderly, the infirm, and the children were also deported, and it therefore became clear that whatever these destinations were, they were not labor camps – still, that these places, certainly Auschwitz and Sobibor, were killing centers, was not yet imaginable.

I stand here at the surviving fragments of the railroad tie where Jews sometimes helped each other, sometimes forced each other aboard trains, aboard cattle cars and passenger cars, bearing healthy Jews, sick Jews, young Jews, and old Jews, with their families and without, with their possessions and identities and contexts and memories stolen from them. Into the gray, sticky morning they rode, over the months, every Tuesday at eleven a.m., one hundred thousand of them departed with a reliability that inspired madness. At eleven on Tuesdays the train left, clacking, clacking, rhythmically, smoothly, delivering its hapless charges mostly to their deaths.

Here I stand, where they once stood, in the same muggy dawn, at the same railway tracks, looking for their traces, for memories of them in this place, in this place where they could not imagine the snarling German Shepherds which were to greet them at Belsen. Thirty-five thousand Jews, on twelve Tuesday train-rides to Sobibor, could not yet imagine their naked run through the chute from registration to gas chamber, could not yet imagine that they would be dead, in Sobibor, within three hours of arrival. So that when you got to Westerbork, and you signed in, you also signed out. You signed out of life; your registration card, although you may not have known it yet, was your death sentence.

Many intuited that indeed they had been sentenced to death, though they did not yet know when the execution would take place, or where, or by what means. What was clear was that life, as it had been understood until now, was over, and that wherever it was that everyone in this transit camp was headed, it was dark there, and bad. At Westerbork, you did the things that people do – you ate, you groomed, you defecated, people beyond despair made love in the open, you may even have studied or taught or worshipped or made beautiful music – but you lived trembling from the roar of imminent death in your ear. You became a desperado prepared to do anything not to get on the lists; mostly, you did what you were told, and often you lost all moral compass. Westerbork was death row without justice; it was a prison in which hope was written off, and where the future, in addition to the past, had been cancelled.

Consider the following excerpt from the remarkable Westerbork diary of Philip Mechanicus:

> "At six o'clock the man came [to the hospital bed] from the Registration Department. 'I regret to have to tell you that your wife is going on the transport this morning. Do you want to go with her . . . ?'

'I want to postpone my decision for a bit.'

The man from the transportation department pulled his watch out of his waistcoat pocket.

'I'll give you another five minutes to make up your mind.'"[1]

The choice here is between suicide and betrayal, between observing the marital covenant and risking almost certain death. Yet what stands out is how the man from the Registration Department (I picture him with his clipboard, quite amiable) assures the patient that he is happy to give him the necessary five minutes, and in doing so shows us how oblivious he is of the parameters of the trial into which the patient has just been thrust. The tone is the same as someone handing out sandwiches: "What'll it be – chicken or turkey?" When, because you have been sentenced, your moral bearings have been blown away, all questions become practical. Depth, sensitivity, meaning, understanding – all this is for the leisurely, those with futures to contemplate.

II

You might have arrived here at Westerbork on a train from somewhere in Holland together with several thousand others – all of you brought to the arrival barrack with its twenty-five symmetrical tables, each staffed by two people, each table bearing one typewriter. Lippmann and Rosenthal, the Nazi Bank, was there, and as you signed away your last assets, you were asked what your profession was. In replying, your profession pulled away from you like the train leaving the station, and you parted

1. Mechanicus, Philip, *Year of Fear: A Jewish Prisoner Waits for Auschwitz*, New York, Hawthorne Books, 1968, p. 40.

with the identity it provided. You simply ceased being who you were. You may have once been a barber, you may have once been a banker, you may have once been a judge. But of course, they came for the judges and for the insurance brokers, the storekeepers, clerks; they came for the homemakers and the mothers and the nurses. The professions, at this moment, anticipated the bodies that later would become ash rising into nothingness in the sky. That past no longer belonged to you, and you no longer belonged to that past. There was only the future now, and the future was deportation and with it, possible, probable, death. It was in this registration hall at Westerbork – the room that doubled, on many a Wednesday evening, as the theater for the cabarets – that your destiny, with the ring of the typewriter bell, was sealed. There were no more rules, notions of escape were delusional; there was no way to survive. Sooner or later everyone would be on a train to Auschwitz.

When you registered in the hall of the twenty-five tables, you understood nothing. You had been thrown out of your home before dawn, brought to a train, and now you were here, outraged. Shoving and being shoved, cursing and being cursed, milling with masses of people you do not know and with whom you surely don't want to be. The three questions: What is this place? What does it have to do with me? What have I done to deserve coming to this place? And if you were younger, or older, a fourth question that eclipsed the others: Who will take care of me?

Day after day, new shipments of Jews arrived here at Westerbork. At the beginning, when the larger Jewish communities were being liquidated, they came in such numbers that a spur needed to be added to extend the tracks that until then had only reached as far as the nearby town of Hooghalen. On one occasion, ten thousand people arrived in a single transport. The camp had no room for them and they slept under the stars.[2]

Later in the war, groups of Jews whose hiding places were revealed, or people who turned out to be gentile by conversion and not by blood, arrived by the truckload. Most were placed in the punishment barracks, and shipped off almost immediately.

Westerbork was a low-security prison. People were permitted to return to Amsterdam and The Hague for this and that, and there were excursions into the countryside, unsupervised, where prisoners picked blueberries. There were volunteers – Jews not yet arrested, who came to care for the orphans, the youth, and the elderly. Some Jews, no longer able to sit out the maddening wait for when their home would be raided by the SS, came to Westerbork on their own.

III

The Dutch Jewish Council provided what we today call social workers for people selected for Westerbork. One of them was my Uncle Anton, a clergyman of sorts. His job was to comfort people selected for deportation. What in the world did he tell them? Did he buy into the Nazi propaganda that if they were sent to the east, it would be better there? Did he tell them that the war would end soon and that everyone would return home and re-stock their refrigerators? Did he tell them that their death sentences had been decreed, and that they may as well make the best of it? Did he speak about Rabbi Akiva and the glories of martyrdom? Or did he teach them to fight despair at all costs, to keep the fires of life and freedom lit, and never to give up? Uncle Anton, the *mohel*, the widower, together with his four children,

2. Ibid, p. 56

49

*Uncle Anton in The Hague, circa 1941, performing a wedding. As I write,
the bride is still alive and well, living in California. She and her husband
both survived the war; he passed away recently. Anton was gassed to death in
Sobibor, together with his four children. Note the yellow star on Anton's robe.*

Isaac, age 11, Judith Hadassah, age 10, Shulamith Ruth, age 8, and
Ben Zion Baruch, age 6 – all ran nude down the chute in Sobibor,
where, on July 9, 1943, they were gathered into the gas chamber.
The powerlessness of it all – a father in his thirties, huddled naked
with his four children, waiting for the gas. I have met people
who remember him, and they say he was a pious man. So as the
Angel of Death entered the room, I cannot imagine but that he
proclaimed his faith in the God of Israel, aware and proud of
their martyrdom, while at the same time wondering about what
the theologian Emil Fackenheim later called the anti-miracle: "In
every generation," the Passover Haggadah reads, "[our enemies]
stand to destroy us, and the Holy One, blessed be He, saves us
from their hands." Not this time.

But Uncle Anton, why was it that I was saved?

Was God, too, powerless in this moment? I think not – yet in Anton's pathetic death scene, disrobed and panicked, inhaling the carbon monoxide, suffering the deepest humiliation ever inflicted on humanity, the incapacity to rescue one's children – can we not ask along with Abraham, "Shall the Judge of all the earth not do justice?" What would it have taken for Him to inflict on the SS and the Wehrmacht what He once rained down upon Sodom and Gomorrah?

I have no memory of Anton, but I do have an alarming photograph of him. We could have been twins. I resemble him physically far more than I do my father.

IV

Arrival at Westerbork. Chaos among the thousands of suitcases and bags, the flotsam and jetsam of a past that has been cancelled. Fatigue beyond fatigue, you have not slept, you have abandoned all interest in your appearance, an interest, in many cases, never to be recovered.

Eventually you are shown to your barrack. Several hundred people in a cramped space, men at one end, women at the other. The metal cots are three tiers high, there is constant struggle for a place for one's possessions, under the tiers, on the cots. Because of the mud of the heath on which Westerbork rests, the floors are always filthy. Imagine the Dutch, unable to get things clean. In the hospital, disease spreads because the sheets and pillowcases cannot be adequately laundered. The humidity in the room leaves everyone in a sweat; the stench of a thousand bodies of all ages trying to sleep is intolerable. And the noise, the noise is unlike anything anyone has ever experienced before – noise intolerable not because it is loud, but because it doesn't let up. Constant coughing, constant shuffling to get to the toilets, children crying – the nights are no longer yours. Lost is the capacity to be alone with your thoughts, lost is your very ability to consider your life. All human struggle, all human thought, all acts of consideration diminish and are displaced by a single goal, a goal of survival, of the scheming, however futile, that survival here takes: making sure not to get on the Monday night lists.

On Monday nights, in each of the barracks at Westerbork, they read the lists of who would be on Tuesday morning's train to the east. Whatever else, you did not want to be on that list. When the names were read, faithfully on Monday nights, some screamed, some attempted suicide, some went stoically, and some went calmly because, as noted, choice and future and management of their lives had already been appropriated from them at registration. There was nothing to be done really, except prepare a blanket or two and a snack.

"Before I went to bed on Monday nights," HR, an old Westerbork survivor told me in 2009, "I folded my jacket on my bed, not knowing whether my name would be called. In one of its side pockets I placed a sandwich; in the other, my *tefillin*."

Westerbork. Where only the elderly and the children died. Babies failed to thrive in Westerbork, although they and their mothers were fed. Children in a camp population of several thousand died at a rate of fifteen per day. What nurturance they absorbed here seemed linked more closely to death than to life. I was one of those babies.

Why did I thrive and not they?

v

Running the camp meant filling trains on Tuesday morning with the quota received from The Hague, usually between one and four thousand people. The Commandant really didn't care who was on the train, so long as it was filled, and he received a great deal of help in preparing the lists from a committee of German Jews.

And so it was that if you were a Jewish doctor, involved in running Westerbork's hospital, and you could decide who was admitted as a patient, you were deciding who for now would not be on the Monday night lists. You were deciding, at least for now, who would live and who would die. And so it was that if you were a Jew in charge of organizing a work detail, that is, if you were handing out jobs, you too were deciding who was not on the Monday night lists – you were deciding, at least for now, who would live and who would die.

And so it was that there was a committee of German Jews that met each week to draw up the lists, to fill the trains, and send their fellows to their deaths. Did they know their fellows were being murdered at their destinations? Were they corrupt? How could they not be? Did they dress like Nazis and affect Hitler's mannerisms? How could they not? Were they fat, and overfed, and oversexed? How could they not be?

To have been in Westerbork is to have witnessed the emptying of Holland of its Jews, an exercise of collusion and collaboration with evil which has almost no equal in history. The collaborators were Dutch citizenry as a whole, which like almost no other European nation, exposed and betrayed its Jews, and facilitated their collection to Westerbork. The collaborators included the Jewish Council, which identified the Jews for the Nazis and helped locate them for deportation. The collaborators were many of the German Jews in Westerbork. In the words of the historian Jacques Presser,

"[Westerbork] was organized in a unique manner: it was managed almost entirely by the German-Jewish inmates themselves, who had taken the initiative in this in an early stage so as to avoid the intervention of the dreaded SS. Because of this the Germans needed only the absolute minimum of guard personnel. Obviously they only allowed this situation to exist because the Jewish camp organization proved to be entirely satisfactory in the matter which was of prime importance to them: the deportation, without difficulties or fuss, of about 100,000 German Jews. The Jews themselves did this so perfectly that the Germans were able to make staffing economies running perhaps into hundreds. In practice, this meant collaboration, barely disguised and degrading, with an increasingly small number of Jews trying to save themselves by sending away larger and larger numbers of their own people. . . ."[3]

This devastating judgment Presser later modifies. In a film about his life, he says the German Jews of Westerbork were good people who made very poor assessments of the situation which yielded poor administrative decisions. They thought cooperation with the Nazis would yield better results for Jewish survival. The most costly error anyone has ever made.

Mechanicus extends the problem:

"Yesterday another small transport came in from Amsterdam, including about 100 cases who had been in hiding. Their heads were shaved and they were given prison clothing. The agents of Lipmann and Rosenthal

3. Jacques Presser, Introduction to *Year of Fear*, op cit., p. 6.

are also playing a new part in relation to these Jews. They pump them to find out the addresses where they have been in hiding. The Jews are behaving worse than shamefully – nearly all of them give the names and addresses for their hosts and benefactors quite readily. . . ."[4]

Appalling as it sounds, and even though it comes from a prisoner who manages to sustain his ethical standards, I think this kind of incident has more to do with the chaos I have described that met the arrivals at Westerbork than with moral choices.

My own inclination is to go with Ety Hillesum's assessment: "You cannot keep everyone back as being indispensable to the camp, or too sick for transport, although you try it with a great many."[5]

Dear reader, do not judge these Jews. They have been moved only now from the deeply silent attics and cellars in which they have been concealed for long periods of time, into the mayhem, the maelstrom, and the mystery that was Westerbork. They have been sentenced to death and with this sentence their moral compass has been, for the most part, disengaged.

The Jews placed in charge of the transportation lists had to choose between sending their own children to Auschwitz or those of their friends. Slowly, slowly the top Jewish officer started to sport a Hitler moustache and walk with a riding crop. Slowly the despised Jewish police force at Westerbork starting displaying Teutonic mannerisms and marches. Slowly these identities started to take. See, the Nazis could now say, the Jews are no different, no better than us. We do it to Jews, but they

4. Ibid, p. 119.

5. Etty Hillesum, *An Interrupted Life* and *Letters from Westerbork*, Henry Holt and Co., New York, 1996, p. 247.

themselves do it to their own brothers and sisters and children. Be patient, watch – Jews too can become perpetrators.

VI

The secret of Westerbork's "success" in deporting Holland's Jews lay not in fear and terror, although these cards could be played when necessary, but in sustaining the ambiguity of what travel "to the east" meant, and Westerbork's last Commandant was the inscrutable master of achieving and sustaining this ambiguity.

Albert Konrad Gemmeker, he with the SS uniform, with the dog, with the mistress, with the whip, with the cottage that still stands, the only intact memorial at Westerbork – Albert ran the camp, together with less than half a dozen German Nazis, and a few Dutch police. There was a world-class hospital in the camp with a thousand beds and teams of doctors and nurses. The hospital, its business and energy, were a ruse meant to prove that the Nazis of Westerbork cared for their charges, and that murdering Jews could not possibly have been the end-game. What would have been the point of healing people in the best clinics, and then sending them to their deaths? Answer: To create an illusion of care, an atmosphere of calm (collecting blueberries unsupervised) so that they would board the trains peaceably; to make the liquidation of Dutch Jewry a quiet, cooperative affair. Albert was masterful in appearing calm but firm, caring but disciplined.

"May we use one of the rooms for a religious service?" my friend Shlomo S., at the time a youth of 17, asked Albert. Albert thought about it, and soon answered in the affirmative.

Albert? Albert was nothing if not courteous, he was not fat; he did not sneer, for the most part; he did not, by his hand, kill

Jews; he presented himself to others as the catalyst, not the cause; he was the middleman, an enabler, not a murderer. He simply expedited the emigration of most of the hundred thousand Dutch Jews to their deaths with firmness, with method – dare I say it – with grace. In his Dutch trial after the war, Albert received ten years, seven really, with three years deducted from his sentence for time already served. He returned to Dresden and resumed his life with his family, gentleman that he was, the mistress forgotten, the cottage abandoned, retaining some of his Jewish friends, arguing to the end that he had no idea what the Jews were being sent to.

Subsequent research, well after his death, shows that he was perfectly aware.[6]

VII

I stand in this forsaken spot where the lupines, planted so many years ago by the German Jews, are still thriving. A place incapable of calling up a memory – because of my age during my inter-ment here, and because, other than Albert's inaccessible cottage, there is nothing left from those days. In vain I sniff for the sharp and putrid smell of latrines, often unbearable.[7] In vain I search for the barracks that were, the large wooden huts that served as the antechambers of death for almost all of Dutch Jewry. I am here to understand not just what the Nazis did, but to know the betrayal and abandonment that occurs when one Jew sends another's children to Auschwitz in order to save his own, and

6. See Ad van Liempt, *Hitler's Bounty Hunters: The Betrayal of the Jews*, Berg Publishers, Oxford and New York, 2005, p. 80.
7. *Year of Fear*, p. 103.

how it was, how it was, that to the best of my knowledge, not a single rabbi spoke out.

Do not judge, dear reader, do not judge your fellow until you have stood in his shoes.[8] When your identity, your assets, your parenting capabilities, your profession, your capacity to choose, have all been taken away, and you have to decide between the survival of your children or your brothers, do you really know what you would have done? And what if you, as rabbi or layperson, simply couldn't believe – didn't imagine as the poet Abba Kovner did in another setting – that all the trains were headed to death?

Was there a way to *interpret* Westerbork when you were there? What could one make of the arrival of all the children from the orphanage in Amsterdam? Groggy, deep in the night, incapable of registering themselves, calmed by their teachers and guardians. What sort of madhouse was this place? If murder is not imaginable, what purpose could be served in bringing them here, to fill these nerve-straining barracks, to walk these aimless streets? What was the purpose of bringing to Westerbork the entire pitiable populations of the homes for the elderly and of the Jewish insane asylum? And what possible end could be served by sending them to the East?

It was in looking at these children, at the old and the infirm, at the parents who realized that in not being able to rescue their children they were betraying them – it was in such lapses of the human spirit that the inmates of Westerbork became aware of their impotence and began to understand their helplessness. It was in the design of this despair that Albert was a master; it was in such humiliation that he excelled. He killed the spirit, and

8. *Pirkei Avot, 2:4*

in so doing, the capacity for physical resistance. He murdered Jewish souls, and left the murder of the hapless bodies inhabited by these souls to his colleagues in the East.

Two groups were not taken in by despair. The first, and I suspect the larger of the two, was the Zionist teenagers. They framed the Holocaust simply as preparation for their inevitable move to Israel and refused to consider other interpretations of their plight. They gathered in Westerbork and Bergen-Belsen, sang the songs of the pioneers of Palestine, and notwithstanding the horrors of their day-to-day suffering, were unflappable in their focus and sense of purpose. Around eighty percent of this group survived.[9]

The second was the *haredim*, the pious orthodox Jews, for whom it was not unusual to spend up to an hour a day in deeply serious Torah study, who in principle never attended any of the cabarets, and who avoided eating cooked food so as not to violate the kosher laws. They did not seem to participate in the hysteria of Westerbork, and attended their incarceration with great shrewdness and extraordinary self-sufficiency. One described to me his bar mitzvah in Westerbork, he spoke to me also of daily religious services (*minyanim*) around the cots in the barracks. He spoke to me of Torah lectures (*shiurim*) by the rabbis in Westerbork, which absolutely did not address the tragedy of the hour, but focused, to everyone's deep relief and appreciation, on matters of Jewish law. In this way, few of them fell deeply into the despair and helplessness that was Westerbork.

9. This is the central argument of the book between *Darkness and Light: 60 Years After Kristallnacht* by Shlomo Samson, Rubin Mass, Jerusalem, 1998.

VIII

And so it is that I stand today in Westerbork, in the first decade of the twenty-first century, at a reunion of survivors, of righteous gentiles who hid Jews, and children of both groups.

Dutch schoolchildren have also been brought here for the occasion. There are speakers parked every thirty yards, whispering in seamless bass tones the names and ages of the victims. A warm sun emerges from a gray sky and settles over the manicured lawns. A small regiment of uniformly-dressed guides (black shirts, trousers, earphone and microphone, sunglasses so their eyes are obscured, they are unrecognizable), do not look at you but motion in the direction of the Camp which is a mile from the Memorial Center. The crowd gathers at the edge of the remaining railway tracks where the trains once stood. The mood is a cross between Churchill Downs (blazers are in) and a nature reserve.

The old Westerbork lunch bell has been preserved; a name is read, the bell is rung. Our charges are clueless that bells are inimical to Jewish memory, that they call-up Christian persecution of Jews, of pogroms. The acoustics of the Holocaust. After the program, elderly survivors are taken out for dinner, where they are served pork.

IX

An old rabbi speaks, asking in tearful tones, how was it possible, how was it possible that 102,000 men, women, and children disappeared seamlessly into the night from this place, without a shot being fired? How could protest, where there was any, be so pitiable and ineffectual, and how could God, too, be among the bystanders?

I survived because God sent His angel to be at my side, I repeat to myself.

While my gratitude to Him is incalculable, somehow it doesn't comfort me a bit.

CHAPTER FOUR

Bergen-Belsen

*W*e departed for Bergen-Belsen from Westerbork on February 1, 1944, and remained there until early April, 1945.

When we arrived at Bergen-Belsen, there was food enough for the 8500 Jewish prisoners in the Star Camp ("Sternlager" in German, so-called because it was a warehouse for prisoners who were thought to be of some exchange value for Germany at the end of the war. These prisoners did not wear the striped camp uniform, but their own clothes, which of course still bore the yellow star; hence the name Star Camp.)

By the end of 1944, seeing that it was losing the war, Germany started closing most of its camps, and in the deep winter, began evacuating the surviving prisoners on foot. These evacuations became known as the Death Marches. Many marches were headed to Bergen-Belsen, which soon held over 40,000 prisoners in its midst, with no increase in food, water, or shelter, and most importantly, no increase in sewage-capacity and sanitation. A Hungarian woman I knew who marched from Auschwitz to Bergen-Belsen told me that her first impulse in arriving at Bergen-Belsen and looking around, was to comment that Auschwitz had been by comparison more tolerable, and that she would have been better off staying there.

In a separate part of Bergen-Belsen, thousands of Russian soldiers were held prisoner in what, if you can imagine it, were even worse conditions. Much of today's Memorial at the site of the Camp is devoted appropriately, it seems to me, to their story.

The central humiliating activity in Bergen-Belsen, among many, was an exercise called the Appel, in which, first thing in the morning and regardless of the weather or one's physical condition, one lined up for hours for the purpose of being counted by the camp administration.

One of the prisoners who arrived in Bergen-Belsen from the death marches was Anne Frank. I do not remember her, of course, but Mother said she did, and that she knew the Frank family from Amsterdam. I mention Anne Frank because I have always wondered how her book might have ended had she lived to add a chapter about her experiences in Auschwitz and Bergen-Belsen – what, in particular, she might subsequently have said about our man's basic and reliable humanistic impulses. Of course, it was not to be, and among scores of thousands of others, she succumbed there to typhus and hunger.

DANCE OF THE CORPSES

Unlike Westerbork, Bergen-Belsen's story is well-known and I limit my remarks on it to questions about its memorialization, about how some dealt with it, and how it survives in some people's insides. (I refrain from using the word "memory" here).

The Holocaust is an unchoreographed dance of the corpses. They are everywhere, from the gutters and collection-wagons of the ghettos to the thirty-thousand dead the British were left to bury in Bergen-Belsen. People, people whose souls have left them, hanging and dangling with expressionless mouths open, with eyes wide and unseeing and empty, bodies unburied, exposed too long. That those around them, only marginally more alive, had to interact with them, to have them perpetually in their field of vision, and in the end, to become immune to them, to see them and not to see them, this is the Holocaust. We children, I the toddler, played hide-and-seek among the stacks of corpses in Bergen-Belsen. This is the Holocaust.

Whereas in Westerbork, the Holocaust, somewhat concealed, played out unseen before us, in Bergen-Belsen nothing was left to the imagination. Whereas in Westerbork, through bureaucratic paperwork and Monday night lists, we sacrificed the children of friends to save our own, in Bergen-Belsen, at the end, when food had disappeared for weeks, we finally *consumed* those sacrifices. My friend ML, who was in Bergen-Belsen when I was, and who is seven years older than I, invariably speaks first, when he speaks of the Holocaust, of the cannibalism he witnessed in the Camp's last insane weeks, when food was long gone and people died while talking to you. The faces of the cooks, he tells me, were calmly passive. Perhaps, I think, like those of the corpses in their dance of total submission and passivity, where limbs no longer protest the directions they take. The living imitating the dead.

To gaze at a corpse is inimical to Jewish values. The law requires burial to be before the sun sets on the day of death. To wash the dead, to prepare them for burial is considered the greatest privilege within the Jewish community, limited to a few of the most pious; the ritual is carried out with the deepest respect and in full silence. In Warsaw, as in the early stages of some of the other ghettos, it was still possible to attend to the dead with some dignity, but in Bergen-Belsen, where the dead almost outnumbered the living, this was no longer the case.

Today the dance of the corpses has not ended. They continue

Sieg Mandaag, the seven year old son of a The Hague diamond cutter wandering about the 15,000 corpses still unburied in Bergen Belsen. Historians have pointed out that the bodies do not seem to be of interest to him. He is four years older than me. (Used with permission from Getty Archives.)

their contortions virtually in the photographs of the ghettos and in the films the British shot at the so-called liberation of Bergen-Belsen, immortalized, if that is the word, in Alain Renais' *Night and Fog*. What shall we say to observant Jews? Gaze not at these expressionless faces and immodest bodies out of respect? Or, as has been our wont – burn these images into your eyes and hearts so that man's cruelty to man never be forgotten; never mind the exposed breasts, never mind the meatless buttocks.

ACCOMPANIED BY THE ANGEL

ME: Tell me, O divine representative, tell me, on the days before the British entered Bergen-Belsen when the camp and its outskirts were strewn with *miles* of Jewish corpses, dressed and undressed in numbers that no eye could apprehend, when never was the humiliation of the Jewish people greater, tell me – did the ministering angels still chant their morning hymns to His Glory? Or did He silence them as He did Israel at the Sea, asking us not to sing when His creatures were drowning?

ANGEL: Such information is not shared with mortals. But what do you think?

ME: I think that when His people are humiliated, so is He. But evil and catastrophe do not make creation any less a marvel, they do not vitiate His Kingship over the world, and the birds continue to sing at dawn, even in Bergen-Belsen.

CEDARS OF LEBANON

This is what S.A. told me about his mother in Bergen-Belsen:
    She is caught taking a piece of bread from the hand of a corpse. In Camp law, this constitutes stealing.

She is brought to "trial." The judges and lawyers are all Jews – before the war, stars in their profession. The Nazis attend the trial for their own amusement.

The prosecution asks her whether she is aware of her "crime," tries to get her to talk about it. She is completely silent.

The defense asks whether she has anything to say on her own behalf; perhaps there was some extenuating issue. She is completely silent.

The judge warns her that if she says nothing, the law presumes her fully guilty and exacts the severest penalty – three days without food in a solitary underground cell. She is completely silent.

Three days later she emerges from the cell, more dead than alive. Her husband, outraged, greets her. "How can you have done this, how can you, in your already weak condition, have done this? Don't you know that it is forbidden to place oneself into danger? Why didn't you answer those questions?"

She responded: "The judge was a Jew – he sat there with his pad, his pencil poised. The lawyers were Jews – they sat with their pads, with their pencils poised. It was the holy Sabbath. Had I spoken, I would have caused each to write and thereby to desecrate the Sabbath. I was not prepared to do that."

Yes, dear reader – of course, her action was wrong; one may not risk one's life to obey the commandments. Had she asked a rabbi, he would have insisted that she speak at that trial. Yet what holds us spellbound in this tale is how her identity remains unassailable, remains impermeable to the assault of the corpses, to the hunger, and especially to the mockery of law that the trial itself was.

ELIJAH THE PROPHET

"I spoke English today," I proudly told Mother, on returning home from my first day of school in Montreal, late in December of 1948, to the teacher, Mrs. George. The one who wears ties.

"But you don't speak English yet," she replied. "Maybe you spoke Dutch and thought it was English."

"I spoke Dutch at first," I replied. "I told the Mrs. George in Dutch that I had to go to the bathroom. She didn't understand, so I pointed to my pee-pee, and she understood right away. One of the other pupils took me to the bathroom but didn't wait outside. When I came out, I was completely lost. I didn't know how to get back to my room. I saw an older girl and told her I was lost. She asked me the room number of my class. That's when I spoke English! I told her Room 19."

"How do you say room 19 in English?" Mother asked.

"Zimmer neunzehn," I replied brightly.

Mother started to cry.

"Why are you crying?"

She cleared her throat, as she always did when she was going to say something important. "'Zimmer neunzehn'" is not English, it's German."

"But I don't know German!"

She began counting with me from one to twenty in German, the voice catching in her throat.

THE MASCOT

He must have been an SS officer of some kind, more advanced than a guard. He had taken a shining to Mother, and, it seems, to me. I became his mascot. Every morning he collected me from Mother's hut, and brought me to the Appel, from which Mother, because of her advanced arthritis, was exempt. I sat on his shoulder during the counting, she related to me. When he brought me back, Mother said, she would find me counting rhythmically: *einz, zwei, drei.* . . .

"It was not a given," she later said, "that when he collected you in the morning, I would ever see you again. But he always brought you back, together with two bottles of milk."

"What was his name?" I asked.

She would not answer.

No survivor remembers me as a mascot at the Appels in Bergen-Belsen. But Mrs. P remembered something else. A year or two before she died, she told me, "Yes, yes; your mother had two bottles of milk each day, and only needed one. I worked in the bakery and got two loaves of bread each day. I would give your mother a loaf of bread, and she gave me a bottle of milk, and that's how, that's how our families survived."

"How did my mother get the bottles of milk?"

She no longer remembered.

THE CORPSES HAVE OVERWHELMED THEM

There was another tale Mother told, about some kind of *aktion* in Bergen-Belsen: a liquidation, it seems, of children. She heard about it and called him immediately; he found me, assisted in his recovery by a birthmark on my back, and returned me to her.

The historians at Bergen-Belsen have never heard of such a liquidation, yet Mother never manufactured tales. What happened there, and what made me worthy of this rescue, that I might retell it again and again?

Somewhere, in a book, I have a group photograph of the staff at Bergen-Belsen, wearing their military caps and long Nazi coats. One of them must be him, I tell myself. I wish I knew which one. I want to call his family and give them something to be proud of.

I look at the photograph and imagine what lies beyond the camera they are staring at. What a question: corpses, of course, in their madness, thousands of them in their macabre dance. The Germans are losing the war; there will have to be explanations. They lack the resources, the time to burn them, to hide them like they did at Treblinka and Belzec.

The corpses have overwhelmed them, there are by now too many to hide. It is the corpses, in the end, that will tell the world what the Holocaust truly was; it is the corpses, long after they are finally buried, in the mounds of earth in which they now rest and in the photographs and films they continue to inhabit, that stare at the Third Reich and all its accomplices, and say – *we* are what you have wrought. We are the testimony. We shall rise again whenever this ghastly tale needs to be recited.

CHAPTER FIVE

The Lost Transport

APRIL 1945: About a week before liberation, the command of Bergen-Belsen decided to transfer the entire section of the camp known as the Sternlager to Theresienstadt. The Sternlager prisoners were ostensibly of some political consequence and, the Nazis reasoned, might prove useful as exchange-barter for German nationals abroad. Three trains were used for this procedure, each headed toward Theresienstadt.

The story of the Sternlager transports is as follows. The first train left the Bergen-Belsen rail platform on April 6, 1945, with 400 inmates of the Sternlager and some 2,100 other prisoners. On April 13, at the town of Farsleben (near Magdeburg), it was liberated by the Americans. The second train, made up largely of Hungarian Jews, left for Theresienstadt on April 7, and actually reached its destination. On April 9, approximately 2,500 remaining members of the Sternlager boarded yet a third train, and this train, as far as anyone in the outside world knew, dropped off the face of the earth and became known to historians as the "Lost Transport."

Only later was it learned that the third train had traveled farther and farther east, searching furtively for rail corridors south to Prague and Theresienstadt that had not been bombed out or occupied by Allied forces. Even after Bergen-Belsen was liberated on April 15, the train remained firmly in Nazi hands – a microcosm of the Holocaust which had already ended, at least by some definitions, in most of Europe. While the British were setting up camp in Bergen-Belsen and attempting to feed and heal its wretched survivors, the train, with its conscientious SS command, hurtled doggedly eastward. With raging typhus, hunger, thirst, and the mounting death toll, the conditions on board were beyond description. The Allies added injury to insult by strafing the train, especially during its frequent stops.

On April 23, the train reached its final destination in a delicate forest deep in eastern Germany, outside the village of Troebitz, where it was liberated, in another ironic twist of history, by a Cossack division of Marshal Zhukov's army. By the time all the dead had been buried, fewer than 2,000 survivors remained to attempt to put their lives back together in this picturesque village-on-a-lake of 700 people where no Jew had ever lived, and many of whose inhabitants had either fled the Russians or were now evacuated by them to provide housing for the Sternlager survivors.

Until July 1945 (by which time almost all had left), the three principal activities that filled the survivors' lives were finding food, recuperating, and burying the endless victims of typhus. These included some nineteen of the town's own burghers and its mayor, who had contracted the dreaded disease from their visitors. Yet among those alive today, testimonies about those months in Troebitz are surrounded by a peculiar haze. While survivors recall people and events in the Sternlager with great precision, memories about the summer of healing in Troebitz remain almost entirely without texture.

My mother, father, and I (not yet three years old) were on this Lost Transport, and 50 years later, at the very end of April 1995, I was invited by a recently formed group, the "Lost Transport Victims Memorial Society," to join a journey of remembrance starting in Amsterdam, pausing in Bergen-Belsen, and winding its way to Troebitz where a memorial wall bearing the names of the victims would be unveiled. I was also asked to address the group when it arrived in Bergen-Belsen. In what follows, the material in italics consists of somewhat amended excerpts from that talk.

With the Jewish memorial in Bergen-Belsen at my back, the sun in my eyes, and a sharp wind blowing my manuscript around, I recite my words. Four busloads of Troebitz survivors and their families gaze unsmilingly at me. Nearby lie the mass graves of Bergen-Belsen in unbearably neat mounds, with legends reading, typically, "Here rest 5,000 dead." I feel an enormous fatigue. It seems to me that evil wants to rest, and I am somehow disturbing it.

We survivors are getting old, and as the end of our days draws near, we find that instead of receding into time, the Holocaust, notwithstanding that it occurred over 50 years ago, seems to draw nearer.

As we move closer to the destiny we ourselves were then spared, as we prepare to join our relatives and friends in the darkness of that Night and in the light of that darkness, the Holocaust, instead of fading, seems to beckon us. It haunts the fullness of our hearts when we sit in our dwellings, when we walk along our way, when we lie down, and when we rise up.

It sits not in the center of our perception, but at the periphery. Like the angel of death, it lurks. Whether our eyes are open or whether they are closed, the Holocaust waits for a momentary distraction, and then it appears. Not far from the daily work of our hands, not far from the play-noise of our children and grandchildren, sits the delirium, sits the typhus; not far, the hunger; not far, the trains.

No danger, then, of the Holocaust being forgotten. Memory, these days, at least for us, is not at risk. It is omnipresent. Sometimes it even feels as though it would take over experience. Sometimes we have to fight to continue living in Amsterdam and Boston and Jerusalem instead of in Westerbork, Bergen-Belsen, and Troebitz.

And so, even as the Holocaust has begun to revisit us, we have decided to come here and revisit it.

On the last day of our journey, an American survivor in her seventies approaches me. "Your speech bore right into my heart," she says. "Do you want to know how I spend my Sundays in America? Not with my family, which is big, appreciative, and loving. No – I go to the Holocaust memorial in our town, which is indoors, and sit near the names and the memorabilia. There, somehow, I am in my element; there, believe it or not, is where I feel most at home."

We are here, then, not just to remember the dead, whom we remember every day. We are here to remember the living. We are here to remember ourselves: to remember who we were in those days, and what it was we went through.

Where the memorials and mass graves are, is not where the Sternlager was, I was told. The place that today is Bergen-Belsen throws memory into disarray. Bergen-Belsen the concentration camp was burned to a crisp by the British to prevent further spread of the typhus from which my father later died, and to show that an era of evil was over. But how wrong they were! Their flamethrowers destroyed any visual clues to jog our memories.

To visitors, the mass graves bring wells of tears, but survivors, who know what happened, who were part of the horror, have trouble distinguishing between history and nightmare – such survivors are not helped by these harrowing mounds, or by the photographs in the Bergen-Belsen documentation center, or by the empty green fields that now form the heart of where the deepest mud and the greatest squalor on earth once reigned. Nor did the British flames end the evil of the Holocaust. For the survivors on this journey, while the Holocaust of history was over, the Holocaust of memory has grown stronger each day.

We are here to testify not merely to the mass murder, but to our own experiences. We are here to see if it all happened the way we remember it, or – for some of us with the amnesia of childhood or the amnesia that comes from too much horror – we are here to see whether it happened the way we were told it happened. And we are more than aware that in reviewing this episode of our lives, we could be changing the way we remember it, and the way we will tell it to our children.

We are here to see whether the biographies we have been telling (and not telling) are true, for we are haunted by the question of – how could they be true?

How is it possible that I, less than three years old in Bergen-Belsen, survived it? Surely I am a fraud, the victim of a liar's tale – a tale about which I remember nothing, yet which I somehow feel doomed to repeat?

Dr. Thomas Rahe is the young, astute, unsentimental German historian whose efforts have gone far to make the documentation center at the present site of Bergen-Belsen a place where – at least with lists of names and numbers – reality and history can in fact be checked. He and I find each other walking along the railway platform. "Close to 600 children survived Bergen-Belsen," he points out to me, "due to its better conditions before 1945.

Six hundred is more than any other concentration camp. The Bergen-Belsen children will be the last survivors, the last to be able to testify to what the Nazis wrought." He is seeking, he tells me, to make his list of child survivors as complete as possible, and urges me to get others to register with him.

We child survivors change the iconography of the Holocaust. We are not small and gaunt, with dark heads and shadows under our eyes, or blond and overweight like many of the older survivors of Auschwitz I have come to know. Most of my fellow child survivors seem to know no Yiddish. They speak English and Dutch and Hebrew without accents. They are breezy, they have a light touch; the shadows from which they emerge, and to which they often retreat, are for the most part imperceptible.

How could the tales be true? How is it possible to survive the filth, the hunger, and the cold? How is it possible to survive the humiliation? We are here not merely to testify to the reality of one another's experience; we are here to examine our reluctance to testify.

We don't want to testify, because our bodies and souls were not created to witness such scenes, our minds not fashioned to contain them, much less to recall them.

We don't want to testify, because every testimony is itself a betrayal: if we were all fashioned as equals, why should they have died and we survived? We can make no sense of how we were selected and not selected; we cannot fathom the explanation, and our inability to explain has led us down a road of guilt; for some, even of shame.

In the end, then, we are here to reflect on why we were given 50 years more than the others, and to consider what we have done with those years.

As the bus moves steadily through the lush German countryside, which is beautiful, yet whose beauty evades me, I move to the front, sit down in the tour guide's jumpseat, and tell my Holocaust tale. Soon others follow, and amid weeping and, surprisingly, much laughter, I discover there are survivors younger than I who remember even less, but who provide me with badly needed doses of reality.

Naturally the older ones remember more. One, about five years older than I, recalls the depths of the hunger, of fighting over potato peels, of stealing and foraging without shame. Another, perhaps ten years older, tells of winter problems: "My shoes collapsed, and they were open at the toes and I got frostbite and was afraid of gangrene. Until I learned that an effective way of treating the frostbite was with the warmth of my own urine."

And stories of enormous dignity: on your birthday, everyone in your family would give you his ration of bread. An SS officer took pity on a child whipped for stealing potatoes, and smuggled him fresh bread. Matzot were baked in Bergen-Belsen for Passover 1944. On the train to Troebitz, which kept stopping, and thereby affording new opportunities to bury the dead, an uncle reminded his nephew of the requirement that the traveler's prayer be recited anew each day, and not merely at the beginning of a journey.

But we are not here, in Bergen-Belsen, merely to speak to ourselves and to one another. We are also here in what has surely become the most contaminated, most wretched spot on earth to speak to God.

For the survivor, speaking to God is perhaps more difficult than it is for others. I have seen survivors pray three times a day in their synagogues and not speak to God; I have seen them teach the deepest secrets of the Torah and not speak to God; I have heard them sing songs of the Sabbath and not speak to God. Only when they recite memorial prayers have I seen them speak to God; in the midst of this inventory of names which no sane mind can apprehend, I have seen them address their Maker. One man I knew would recite the prayer "Lord, full of mercy" for the six children he lost at Auschwitz – one prayer at a time, one child at a time, pronouncing each name carefully and slowly until I was certain the Court of Heaven and the Court of Earth could bear it no longer, and I myself wanted to flee his presence and escape from an accusation from which there was no hiding.

Today, in this place, I will try to speak to God. I will speak only on my own behalf, not merely because I represent no one but myself, but also because there are friends among us who are nonbelievers, and after the Holocaust I have come to feel their ache and to respect their silence.

In the charming town of Bergen we are wined and dined by the Minister of Culture for Lower Saxony. He is calm, remarkably sane and clear, and makes a brief speech. Eighty-five percent of all Germans today, he tells us, were five years old or less during the war. The inheritance our parents left us is the moral squalor that was the Holocaust. Each day Germans need to deal with this inheritance. One way they can do it, he continues, is by putting up money for institutions like the documentation center at Bergen-Belsen, where an effort is being made to list every single one of the 120,000 inmates of the camp, so that, in his words, "the names do not ever lapse into anonymity."

To which I reply:

There is nothing you can do that will ever redeem either your parents or yourselves from the moral squalor you describe. No amount of money, no amount of virtue can ever bring light to the darkness your country has created. The deeds of your parents cannot be forgotten, and as long as memory stirs, as long as the word Auschwitz continues to bring a shudder to the human frame, you are doomed to be their representatives, and your hands will be stained with blood that you yourselves may not have spilled. For as long as people remember history, or hear a Jewish story, or see a Jewish child, you are destined both to take responsibility for this darkness and never, ever to be forgiven for it.

(But of course I say no such thing.)

In Berlin, we are taken on a bus tour of the city. We begin at the zoo, and our guide, who has clearly not been clued-in to her new charges, opens along the following lines:

"Welcome to Berlin. Two-and-a-half hours is a short time to see all the history of this city, but we will do our best. Most bus tours of Berlin begin right here at the zoo, so perhaps I will tell you something about it, to give you a sense of what the city has gone through. In 1939, before the war, Berlin had not one but two zoos, which boasted more than 10,000 animals. In 1945, only one zoo was left, with barely 90 animals. . . ."

A slow titter runs through our bus. Someone needs to fill her in. This is what I tell her:

In 1933, Berlin boasted 172,000 Jews and at least sixteen synagogues. These Jews, unlike the animals, were asked to leave, and so in 1939 Berlin was down to 83,000 Jews. But most of those were murdered, so that by 1945 there were only 5,000 Jews left, and while you still had a zoo, you didn't have a single synagogue. With all due respect, madam, your remarks make me wonder: whom do Berliners miss more, the elephants or the Jews?

(But of course I say no such thing.)

Finally our small armada heads toward Troebitz. Security is tight – there are two police helicopters overhead and our bus, the first in a caravan of four, is preceded by a cruiser with its blue lights flashing and its klaxon blaring. For many, the terrifying come-and-go sound triggers a memory of the Gestapo, and brings us close to tears.

What will Troebitz be like? Will the villagers be there, or will they hide in their attics and peer out from behind drawn shades? Will Troebitz remember us? Will we remember Troebitz?

The survivors spill out of the buses as if they had not been allowed outdoors for months, and gather, for the first time, for a group photograph. The atmosphere is electric, the mood high. This is an event – indeed, a scene – that is not likely to be repeated; a return of incalculable moral vengeance, of great triumph. We the begrimed, the humiliated of the earth, have returned! We lived! We have made something of these all-but-stamped-out lives!

The villagers of Troebitz are present in large numbers: the mayor, a nephew of the one who died of typhus; the store-keepers; the housewives; and most of all, the high-school students. I work with students at home, and I am at once drawn to these. Their faces are exceedingly straight and innocent, though not naive. They look calmly and directly at me; it is clear that they know everything.

Come, they say, come and see our exhibit. In the Town Hall we explore a project composed jointly by the region's high schools: a photographic display, with commentary, of the journey of the Lost Transport, complete with a chilling table-sized model of Bergen-Belsen; photographs of the liberation of a kind which children should not have to see; maps of the railroad routes; and a list of victims buried in Troebitz, including my father.

No Jew had returned to Troebitz for 40 years. In 1985, conscience urged one survivor to see under what farmland his father's grave might lie. What he found instead was an impeccably kept Jewish cemetery; his father's gravestone was intact, maintained as it had been left in 1945, with the flowers tended as if by a member of the family.

"Two thousand people showed up in our village of 700," the mayor tells us. "We didn't invite them, and they didn't want to be here. But we did what we could." Troebitz had remembered us with dignity, and we, as we weep deep tears at the memorial service in the small Jewish cemetery overlooking the lake, we remember Troebitz.

I begin my prayer with a story.

Master of the Universe, You who remembers all things forgotten, remember the little four-year-old boy as he stood in that white hospital room in Eindhoven in 1946. In that big white bed lay an unfamiliar woman, claiming to be his mother. But this could not be his mother! When he had last seen his mother seven months ago on a train in Troebitz, she was a bag of bones weighing 50 pounds, crazy with delirium.

Creator of Heaven and Earth, You before whom there lies only eternity, before whose glorious throne there is no forgetting, remember, I beg You, that moment in the hospital room, where in the presence of the priests and the nuns, the woman in the bed finally succeeds in persuading this child that she really is his mother. Remember how the mother, resisting tears, asks the child to open the drawer in the white night table next to her bed. The child obeys, and there, among a sea of chocolates and candies, he finds his gifts: the small red prayerbook, the ritual undergarment with its fringes.

Do You hear, O Listener to the prayers of Your people Israel – that it never occurred to her to think that You had abandoned her on that dark night? Father of Compassion, You whose eye observes, whose ear hears, You who each day enters the inventory of our virtues in a book, know that this was not an isolated case. Those Jews who were religiously observant before the Holocaust for the most part maintained their observance after the Holocaust.

Master of the Universe, in the night we weep, but in the dawn, do we not sing Your praises?

Lord of Wonders, look upon us – orphaned and widowed, haunted and half-crazed by a night which refuses to end, are we not back? Are there not more students studying Your Torah now than before the night? Do not more Jews speak Your holy tongue now than before the night? Are not our young men and women, especially when they don that green uniform of the army of Israel, every bit as prepared to die for their people as was the generation of the night — who had no choice?

And so, Master of the Universe — You who reigned before aught was created — we the survivors approach You with the great question of the sages about liberation: why is this night different from all other nights? Have we not suffered enough? How long shall we be haunted by the trains and by the typhus? How long will the barking of dogs and the sounds of German bring sweat to our palms? Is not this the darkest night of all? Have we not suffered enough?

Master of the Universe, forgive me if I call upon all who are buried here, and in Troebitz, and in Auschwitz and Treblinka, and in the other mountains of human ash, to join with those of us gathered here today, to form a rally of protest. You in whose hand lies the spirit of every living thing: when will the night finally become the dawn, the memories be given meaning, the nightmares become dreams? When will the Great Sabbath finally arrive, whereon, as You have promised, the lion shall finally lie down with the lamb, and a little child shall lead them?

CHAPTER SIX

Mother, Father
and Other Unfinished Business

Troebitz ends for me with my first secure memory of the Holocaust, by which I mean a memory I am certain of. It is also my worst memory of these years. Mother, as I have said, given up for dead in Troebitz. Father already buried in a mass grave there. And I — I find myself in what I was later to learn was the railroad station in Leipzig, alone, with a sign on my chest bearing my name and nationality. It was raining and very dark. There was only one thought — not where was my mother, not where was my father, but a terror: Who, who will take care of me? This terror of the world has never left me. Deep in my bones, I continue to live with what is contrary to what my mind knows to be different: that the single most important lesson of the Holocaust is that our capacity to take care of each other was taken away from us. As often as I have consoled the bereaved and the stricken, as often as I have accomplished this task myself, still I do not believe that the capacity for people to console each other is an inevitable part of the human experience. The Holocaust has fashioned within me a myth, a false one to be sure, but one from which I cannot recover, and within me remains a three-year old trapped in moral lies.

The train from Leipzig took me to Holland, and this is where my tale picks up.

MOTHER

Spring 1946. I am riding breathlessly on the back of a scooter, my arms wrapped around the broken-in male jacket in front of me, my head buried deep into it, one eye only taking in the colors, the sun. He and his wife had adopted me. I remember only his back – no face, no name. Gloriously we putter through Elysian Fields of golden hay and summer greenery – let this ride never end, I ask. It does, and we arrive at the Catholic hospital in Eindhoven. Gingerly he helps me down, fearful of my pallor, my fragility.

We are in a room. Everything is white. The ceilings are very high. There is a woman in the white bed with the white bars, surrounded by the whole Catholic Church, nuns, priests; there wasn't a lot of room and it was getting hot. Someone signals me to greet her. "Hello madam," I say. The jacket that brought me this far says, "She is not 'madam', she is your mother."

After the Holocaust.

My MOTHER? My whole being rebels at the word, my body shakes. Somewhere inside I scream a cry so grief-struck, so thunderous, that no one is left in the room, save for the woman in the bed. I look at her shattered form, her rheumatic, deformed legs, the Holocaust madness still in her eyes. My mother? Not! I screamed silently, Not! The jacket has left, his warmth, his reassurance puttering into a distance not meant for me. Can a child actually want to die?

After the Holocaust.

"Yozef," she says, "Yozef, yes, I am your mother."

"He doesn't seem to recognize you," the Church says, "it *is* possible that he isn't yours, isn't it? Children get lost, displaced, mix-ups are common. We really cannot let you keep this child unless we are sure he is yours. Whoever he is, you can be sure that the Church will take very good care of him."

She understands the stakes; she always does. That's how we survived.

"Yozef," she says, "Yozef, come here." There is kindness in the horror of her form. I come.

"He doesn't recognize me," she says to the Church, "because the last time he saw me I weighed seventy pounds less than I do now."

"Come sit here," she says to me, "we'll play a little." I want no part of her wretched, morbid form. I don't sit, I feel I'll vomit. I don't understand the Church.

She says to the Church, "There are too many people in this room. How can I reacquaint myself with my child in the middle of a theater? Can you all please leave?"

The Church leaves, save for one or two, ostensibly the decision-makers. She speaks to me with love, gently, gently. "Do you remember how we used to read Little Red Riding Hood together, how I would read one line and you would finish the rhyme in the next line?"

She tries it. I respond haltingly with the rhymes. Soon I cannot control them, they pour out, rhyme after rhyme, verse after verse. *Thus did I sing that morning the poetry of Bergen-Belsen, of the corpses I played around, of the typhus-feces that were my sandbox. Thus did I sing the song of the hunger and of the fever, of the cold that does not let up, of mother washing my body with her coffee rations. Thus did I sing then, on the morrow after the Holocaust, of the rhymes of the angel of death, thus did my song echo the rattle in father's chest as he reached up skyward to call out to his brothers, long gone in Sobibor, that he too was coming . . .*

The Church leaves. There is a drawer in the white, white night table next to the white bed with the white bars. "Open it," she says to me. Inside, a small mountain of foil-covered chocolates. Deep in the mountain, I rescue a small pair of *tzitzis*, and a small, exquisite red *siddur*. "What *are* they?" I ask.

"You are a Jew," she says to me, "and Jews need these things." Our first conversation. After the Holocaust.

FATHER

I moved through dooms of longing for father. After the war, when I came to, when I began to understand the difference between then and now, past and present, the yearning, vast and amidst uncontrollable weeping, began – for a man, a dad, of whom I had no memory.

"Father, Father, Father, where are you?" I would cry into the vast arenas of existence. In a frenzy I searched for him everywhere, in all the uninhabited places I knew he needed to be. There was a photograph of him, clean-cut, sane, pleasant. The expression on it never changed; it never broke into a smile, never left its form, never expressed anguish, not over my absence, not over his. Today it has become affixed, stuck, to the glass of its frame, still unchanging, still unresponsive, deteriorating.

He was one of six brothers and a sister, each upended in Westerbork, each murdered together with spouses, with children, in Auschwitz and Sobibor. Before the war, they would all gather on Friday evenings for Shabbat dinner at my grandparents'

Father circa 1940. A copy of this photo on my mantel-piece is disintegrating before my eyes.

home. They would have a jolly time with each other, Mother reported, especially as they sang the Sabbath table hymns.

Isaac was the *pater-familias*, Father's father, who died before I was born. As a result, unlike all of his children except for Father, he has a grave – in the Jewish cemetery in Scheveningen. He was mercifully spared the knowledge that all of his offspring, every last one of them, was murdered. Rika, Grandmother, was not so lucky, but when she went to her death in Sobibor, she at least knew that some of her children and grandchildren, including me, were still alive. (In the end, I alone was spared.)

Isaac was the principle slaughterer of kosher meat for The Hague. He was known as a quiet man, deeply devoted to his faith and practices, and was seen, more than once, unwrapping his sandwich from its wax paper at public meals where he didn't trust the levels of kosher practice. About her mother-in-law, Grandmother Rika, Mother spoke only in the most venerating tones – about her kindness, her selflessness, the details, the minutiae involved in her care of others.

And then Father, beautiful, enigmatic Father whom I mourned inconceivably and inconsolably for what seemed millennia – Father, with his Mona Lisa expression on a photograph that is self-destructing. On our train out of Bergen-Belsen, the train that was liberated by the Cossacks, he was still alive. He and Mother and I were still together on the train. My first memories have to do with the rattles coming from his faceless chest, with Mother's voice (not faceless) having evolved from soprano to bass (the percussion of the Holocaust) – both of them off their heads, quite mad from delirium, both of them skeletons, scorched with typhus fevers, both of them covered (Mother later said) with potato sack and lice. He died a few days later in Troebitz, where he still lies buried in a mass grave next to the Church. Are the church bells echoes of his chest rattles, of the pneumonias, the millions of pneumonias that were the Holocaust?

In Troebitz he was quarantined in an isolation shack where, a few days later, he died. I don't think Mother knew at the time. I don't think I knew. I don't know how I found out; I don't know who told me, but I sense that whoever it was, I understood and was deeply frightened.

In 1995 I finally revisited Troebitz. The isolation shack in which he died had been demolished only a year earlier. No one consulted me or any other Troebitz survivor about this.

BOOK TWO

AFTER THE HOLOCAUST

CHAPTER SEVEN

The Bijenkorf

Imagine the Bijenkorf (pronounced "Bay-en-korf"), The Hague's largest department store, street level. Imagine towering ceilings braced by pillars wide enough for the people behind them to disappear. Imagine a symphony of flowers, their glorious color now diaphanous, now overbearing. Imagine the orchids, the Dutch tulips fresh each day, the vast bouquets in pots tall enough for me to hide in. Imagine the twinkle of the diamonds in their cases, the sedate gold watches, the silver spoons shaped like windmills. Imagine the gentle, loving fragrances, the hushed conversations, the call to, the reverence for, luxury. Imagine experiencing this as I did in 1947 as a five-year-old child, struggling to take in this world, which seemed neither imaginary nor real.

What reality was reflected in these neat rows of blouses, in the delicate piles of lingerie? What was it about their freshness, their seeming to have arrived into this world without the intercession of human hands, folded into reassuring, gentle order? I have no memory of any men's clothing – or any objects of interest to men, for that matter – from any of these frequent childhood visits with Mother. Visits – not shopping expeditions, mind you. I would have remembered the jingle of the cash registers, the splash of the change into their cash drawers. I would have remembered Mother digging into her change purse, which fascinated me, and I don't.

I stood blinking in the light reflecting off the beveled glass of the counters with their subdued scarves and fingered gloves – I stood there without context, without connection, swept into the rushes of fantasy. As the Bijenkorf drew me not always willingly into its endless invitations to hope and to the imagination, I was never altogether certain as quite to what brought Mother and I there, what brought us there repeatedly. Perhaps I didn't know what "buying" was; perhaps, alarming as this may seem, there was more there than met the eye.

Mother was slow on explanations of what we were doing there, the occasional purchase of yet another pair of butter soft gloves notwithstanding. The Bijenkorf was an admixture, a confusion, a profusion of both high chaos and high order – the celestial heights of its vaulted ceilings adding to its uninterpretability.

I was something of a chatterbox as a child, yet don't have a sense of much talk between us at the Bijenkorf. There was too much, as it turns out, to talk about. The talk was not yet ready, still pre-articulate, still waiting for its moment.

Long after she died in 1982, and certainly before, I found myself spending long hours wandering through department stores, usually alone, filled to bursting with pathos, silently vocalizing the heartbreak arias of *Traviata* and *Boheme*, at the edge of tears, and filled with a loneliness and emptiness no human being should have to endure. Little did I realize on those occasions that it was not yet another tie that I was looking for, that it was Mother – Mother in a feathered hat with a fine-lace veil to her nose, warmly clad, gloves clutched in one hand, and for all her heavy arthritic gait, looking pretty and happy. I expected her to emerge from around corners, in this 1947 get-up, with a grin, ready to take me home.

Never, since the Bijenkorf, could I talk to her, nor she to me. Yet throughout our lives we could serve each other great dollops of validation, of happiness and contentment. Somehow this deep, mutual understanding, sustained long into my adulthood and her old age, hearkened back to what seemed to be those weekly visits to the palatial Bijenkorf, to the energy that entered her there, to the confidence those occasions afforded her. That she could *do* this, that she could be in this glorious spot, is what it was all about.

Let me try and explain:

Alan MacAuslan, one of several medical student volunteers finally headed to Bergen-Belsen some weeks after its liberation in April of 1945 (few doctors and nurses volunteered to go there). He described what he saw when for the first time he entered one of the huts with its typhus-ridden, dying inmates:

"We took a look round – there was faeces all over the floor – the majority of people having diarrhea. I was standing aghast in the midst of all of this filth trying to get used to the smell which was a mixture of post-mortem room, a sewer, sweat and foul pus, when I heard a scrabbling on the floor. I looked down in the half-light and saw a woman crouching at my feet. She had black matted hair, well populated and her ribs stood out as though there were nothing between them, her arms were so thin that they were horrible. She was defecating, but she was so weak that she could not lift her buttocks from the floor and, as she had diarrhea, the liquid yellow stools bubbled over her thighs."[1]

This *could* have been Mother – the physical description fits, the uncontrollable defecation that is the hallmark of typhus fits – but it wasn't. I quote MacAuslan to convey Mother's condition during the months of February and March of 1945. She lay there in Bergen-Belsen on the upper planks of a three-tiered bunk, slithering in her excrement, her shit dripping down onto the prisoners below us, weak to the point where she could barely raise her arms, humiliated by the absence of toilets, and even more, it seemed, by her own helplessness, which continued to plague her for the rest of her life, and which she fought, as she did in Bergen-Belsen, like a tiger. She weighed fifty pounds on the train out of the Camp.

What private imaginary world did she inhabit, in the midst of this "excremental assault"[2] that helped propel her past it, letting her maintain some sense of self, indeed, of a better universe? Later, later in life, when I still couldn't bear hearing about it, she answered this question with a hint of a smile. "I would pretend that I was on the first floor of the Bijenkorf," she would say, "I would close my eyes and smell the flowers."

The outings to the Bijenkorf in 1947–8 involved Mother's transposing one world over another; they constituted the negation of the excremental assault. Overlaying this unspeakable universe now was the orderly and the dignified and the beautiful,

1. MacAuslan, A., "Belsen, May, 1945," *St Thomas's Hospital Gazette*, 43 (1945), pp. 103–7. Cited in Chephard, Ben, "After Daybreak: The Liberation of Bergen-Belsen, 1945," Schocken Books, N.Y. (2005), p. 98.

2. The phrase is that of Terrence des Pres. See the chapter with this title in his "The Survivor," NY Oxford University Press, 1976.

the pre-existent over the parenthesis of whole evil. Each visit, reinforcing the previous one, was the vindication of a survivor who had succeeded, in some measure through her own grit, in forcing imagination and memory to partner in an effort so mighty that the boundaries of heroism itself needed to be re-defined. She had engaged what was precious about the physical world together with what beauty the human imagination could order it into as her weapons against Germany's fecal worldview, and she had prevailed. She had won the Second World War. The Bijenkorf was the theater of the victory celebrations, perhaps the Bijenkorf itself *was* the celebration. So at least during the *days* of those years.

The *nights* were another matter.

★

The visits to the department stores continued well into my eighth year (1950), when we had already moved to Canada. Westerbork and Bergen-Belsen had done little for her arthritis. Her left leg had continued to harden, the joints didn't bend, and she walked – not very well – with a severe and profoundly embarrassing gait that involved her whole body. For an extraordinarily – ideolog-ically – modest woman, the gait was her antithesis. There was nothing immodest about it, but it negated the elegant concert pianist she had been before the war, it negated her claims about how the boys (now all murdered) had fought with each other to walk her home. It negated any possibility of anyone wanting to ever marry her again. It involved a swerve that took her all in, from head to foot, that called attention to her, that was as trying to look at as it was to execute.

I mention this because as the arthritis progressed during these months, I, unconsulted on the matter, was quite deliberately assigned the role of her cane. Her frame leaning comfortably on mine made me feel strong, needed, even a little proud, although the feeling that I'd rather not be doing this never quite left me either. We would arrive by cab at the St. Catherine Street entrance to Eaton's, she with her arm firmly planted on my shoulder, me, as I said, not without some pride in my indispensability. Once again was I absorbed into Eaton's' oak atmosphere of business dignity, yet again internalizing a sense of order, an esthetic that nurtured coherence and civility.

The barriers to Eaton's for Mother were its revolving doors. For starters, she could barely control them as she passed through. Then, too, she and I could not occupy the same segment – not big enough – and creature of habit that I already was, reliably followed two carefully-counted segments behind her. I don't know what it was she held on to walking through it, but somehow, as she liked to say, "we" managed.

Once, though, she didn't. She was almost through, with me two faithful segments behind her, when a powerful push from my rear sent me face-first into the glass partition, and far worse, sent Mother flying out onto the garden-plush dark green carpeting that swathed the street level floor of Eaton's. She lay there horribly, in fetal position, unable, as I swiftly realized, to get up. Nor did I know how to get her up or whether I *could* get her up, and the vast, cosmic helplessness that arose from within me, of the failure, of the humiliation, of its finality, of my shame, flushed my face. Who could help me, I cried inside, and if I can't take care of her who would?

While I stood there trembling, my mouth wide open, the gentleman who had pushed the revolving door too hard gallantly dropped to his knees at Mother's side, and with profuse apologies and bemused coaching from Mother, lifted her gently and helped her sit down on a chair. He took far too much time to do this. He and my mother stared at each other, she charming, he suave and debonair. I knew *exactly* what was going on; the S.O.B. looked exactly like Anthony Eden, whom Mother made no secret of admiring as the handsomest man on the planet. Never did I hate a human being more than this man, this bum who had sent a crippled woman flying with a strength so vastly superior to mine that if I had tried to bite him or something, he would have flicked me off like a fly. This selfsame brute was now attending Mother with poise and with flair, daring to administer compassion, and coming off like some kind of hero.

When it was all over, Mother said something like, "Well, what did you think of all *that*?" My throat was locked like the Jaws of Life. We never returned to Eaton's lest, for me, another social catastrophe present itself. I eventually completely forgot about the Bijenkorf too, and because we never talked about it, I forgot about Bergen-Belsen as well. At least during the day. Nights, as I said, were another story.

CHAPTER EIGHT

After the Holocaust, the Holocaust Continues

Below the proscenium of my childhood, somewhere in my third year, a massive curtain starts to rise. Some gray corduroy of exceptional heft is rolling up perfectly, as if onto a bale for the first time. I alone am on the stage, looking out into the world. With the hiss of the curtain's rise, the darkness of the stage is no more. From here on in, I am privy to all experience, in Technicolor. The amnesias of childhood are finally over. I am not very self-aware. I am old enough to retain memory. No more deleted scenes of Westerbork or Bergen-Belsen. I am able to take in ("apprehend" the philosophers say) the world as my own. The curtain rises to a streaked, flawed dawn.

★

To understand, though, the times in which my mind finally opened up so that memory could form in a coherent, recoverable way, to understand the times, the culture, the background in which Mother and I, but especially Mother, found ourselves facing in those immediate post-war years, allow me to depict in a few lines, the sheer headiness, corruptness, madness and – yes – joyous exhilaration of those days.

Remember that no country in Europe – certainly Western Europe – bore within it such deep and enigmatic contradictions in its politics and ethics, its sadness and joy, and in its guilt and innocence, as did the Netherlands.

Time and again, certainly early in the Nazi occupation, the courageous Dutch stood up to their conquerors. Serious public marches and vigorous protests were organized. An effective Resistance was developed that engaged in all kinds of subterfuge against the German military and the SS, and managed to hide hundreds of Jewish families and close to 5,000 Jewish children.

Yet the population numbers, the death counts, yield another story. Belgium lost 50% of its Jews, even Germany too lost "only" 50% of its Jews. The Netherlands, on the other hand, lost 90% of its Jews. Of 135,000 Dutch Jews, fully a 108,000 were sent off to their deaths: 90% of Dutch Jewry.

In his book, *Hitler's Bounty Hunters*, Ad Van Liempt (Berg Publishers, Oxford/NY, 2005), describes the particular zealotry exhibited by bounty hunters delivering Jews to the SS. In the years directly after the war, these bounty hunters were indeed prosecuted and sometimes executed, but the picture emerging from these legal depositions is in stark contrast to the world of the Resistance, and to the Dutch as a humanitarian nation.

In fact, when the surviving Jews emerged from hiding after the war, or limped home from the camps, and they encountered their old gentile neighbors, they had little certainty as to whether they were meeting friend or foe, hero or villain, supporter or betrayer.

As Judith Miller has pointed out,[1] the Dutch poured millions into the Anne Frank house to give the impression that every Dutchman had been hiding a Jew in his attic, when this was tragically very far from the truth.

Returning Jews, moreover, encountered a Dutch community that in addition to its overall grievous war experience had also faced a massive food shortage in the last year of the war. Thousands had died of hunger, and so, not unlike the Poles, the Dutch saw themselves as victims of the Nazis and not as bystanders – certainly not as perpetrators.

The treatment of returning Jews was awful – some were placed in concentration camps on the Dutch border. Their fellow inmates often included Nazi perpetrators awaiting trial. The Jews were detained until they could prove their Dutch nationality. Others, upon reaching their homes, found their houses occupied by strangers and were permitted only the partial return of their confiscated effects. The Dutch did not seem to realize that treating Jews like regular Dutch citizens and not like a nation scheduled for extermination was itself a form of cruel anti-Semitism.

Moreover, if a Jewish child had been separated from its parents during the war, and these parents had survived, it was not a given in Dutch law that parent and child would be reconciled. On matters of family reconciliation, Dutch law seem to have been written to protect these children from their parents, especially if their parents were Jewish and Dutch courts soon become clogged with hysterical mothers and fathers who just wanted their kids back.

Was this Dutch culture of having to prove parental competency

1. Judith Miller, *One by One by One*, Simon & Schuster, New York, 1990, p. 96.

in order to retrieve your own children utter madness? Was it cruelty beyond cruelty? You come back from Bergen-Belsen, and Theresienstadt, physically and emotionally decimated, having no certainty that anyone in your family is left alive – not even your children. You then engage in what must be history's most desperate, harrowing manhunt for your missing child, and when in some moment of divine grace, you locate your child, the authorities tell you your child is no longer yours – that the child's adoptive parents, who have hidden them all these months and years, are more competent than you are in your laughingly humiliated, compromised and shaken condition, and that these adoptive parents now get to keep your son, your daughter. Such a parent is left feeling that where the Nazis did not ultimately succeed in separating parent from child, the Dutch did.

Even in those cases where the adoptive family is more competent than the hapless returning concentration camp survivors, the cruelty involved in refusing these parents their children, to me, overrides any consideration of "what's best for the children."

If these are the biological parents that God provided these children, then place this moral dilemma at His feet, and do not play His role yourself.

The Dutch Jews, having a growing sense that they were not among friends, began to leave the Netherlands for Israel, the US, and Canada. Before the war Holland had 135,000 Jews; in 1946, there were fewer than 30,000; by 1954, the Jewish population had dwindled further to 26,000.

Against this culture of grief, displacement, and the intolerable loss of vast communities of people, despite a post-hunger culture that hardly brought out the best in people in day-to-day neighborly relations, 1946 was nonetheless a heady time. The Allies had won the war, the Queen had returned to her country signaling the end of the five-year period in which the Dutch had been deprived of their sovereignty – people danced in the streets and the smell of freedom was everywhere. Mother found a few of her surviving women friends, and the three of them brought much pleasure and companionship to each other in those days of exploded society and café life, of street romps, and exponential joie-de-vivre. Albert Camus successfully portrays this joy and its accompanying amorality in his novel *The Plague* when he describes the social behavior that emerges with the dissipation of the plague. It is also surprisingly well depicted in Paul Verhoeven's film (2007) *Black Book*.

★

It must be April 1947, and although the sun is shining, the Dutch spring still feels cold. I am five years old, in The Hague, seated in the large living room of the *Joods tehuis* (pronounced *yode's ta-House*), a place which today we would call a recuperative center; this one is for Jewish survivors of the Holocaust. The intended recuperation is not physical. People in the home have largely recovered from the dreaded illnesses which befell them in the camps. There are no nurses or physicians here, and I remember no wheelchairs. What they are recovering from is the Holocaust itself, from which, needless to say, there is neither recovery nor escape. Their worlds are long shattered, everyone that matters is dead, and the point of going on in a country in which your neighbors betrayed you more extensively than almost any other country in Europe – the point of going on in this land with its inhabitants who avoid your eyes, and with its canceled dreams, is less than clear.

A group home, in which there is no group, in which people retire to their bedrooms silently after dinner. A group home in which the lights go out early, followed by screams and madness.

The *Joods tehuis* has bedrooms upstairs, a kitchen and living and dining rooms downstairs. Of the large group that lived there, a few faces are preserved in my memory, one of which is that of Mr. Levi, who is very serious and very bald and very tall, and who, in his unsmiling way, is very kind to me. We sometimes climb high into the stairwell where a massive oval port window rides inwards on hinges so sensuously smooth that just opening it is a treat. Here Mr. Levi shows me how to toss the pieces of bread high out into the salt air so that, to my great glee, even before they reach the ground, they are swooped up by the seagulls.

During those years in the *Joods tehuis* I was often overcome by fits of hysterical, tear-filled screaming, usually initiated by Mother's mad expectations of me. Fits which I was powerless to stop, and which in turn led Mother to beat me in desperation with the wooden back of a clothes brush I still own. The clothes brush did little for the screaming, and the fits ran a long watery course: my nose filled to bursting and my tears completely drenched my blouse and eyes and face and pillow (a big, starched, pink affair that felt like sandpaper). I could barely see my world through this foggy spray, it smothered me in a blanket of soft acid, leaving my face hot and raw. Sleep could relieve these fits, sleep, and Mr. Levi, who with his calm high-seriousness and his unshakable respect for Mother, managed to steer me back to equilibrium.

★

I am up early this morning, glad to be out of the hard bed Mother and I share. Mr. Levi is the administrator of the *Joods tehuis* and the only other person awake. I am staring at three red balls lying in a clear glass bowl, a fruit knife perched vertically in their midst.

"What are these red balls, Mr. Levi?" I ask.

"Apples," he replies.

"What are apples?"

"A fruit that one eats. Would you like to taste one?"

"Yes."

He takes the knife, and with astonishing dexterity, peels and cuts it, and hands me a slice.

It tastes tart and utterly unpleasant, and I say so. Mr. Levi remains serious.

Mother, I discover later that morning, loves apples. Later in life this knowledge of our differences helps me separate from her.

★

Haya, my age, also lived in the *Joods tehuis*, with her brothers and mother. My memories of her then are indistinct. But when I caught up with her in the United States some sixty years later, I remembered with perfect clarity the explosive heartache I felt when she and her family moved unannounced out of the *Joods tehuis*. I am still able to come close to tears and experience how deeply I grieved for her when I searched for her the morning after they left and could not find her.

★

The child that totters out of Bergen-Belsen denies by his sheer survival that Bergen-Belsen happened. There is no stage entrance for a child amidst the thousands of corpses the British buried there in April 1945, there is no role – the audience wouldn't believe it. Those who survived the hunger and the typhus are often spoken about in theological terms: a miracle, people say. But children? Toddlers like myself playing near the unburied dead are beyond what the mind can assimilate, they veer at the

*Mr. Levi and me in the Home for Jewish Holocaust
Survivors in The Hague, 1947.*

furthest edge where even theology dare not tread. The word
"miracle," however true, here rings inadequate, as theology itself
is inadequate. It is somehow easier for those who look back at
these children to exclaim that it was impossible for them to survive (how often have I been asked incredulously – *you* survived
the Holocaust? How old were you?) than to simply accept this.
For the children themselves it is certainly easier to pretend that
they hadn't been there, that they did not act in their own drama,
that their story belonged to others, perhaps to those who did
remember.

★

What then does it mean to be a witness to such an event which you don't remember, especially amidst the urgency that you may be its last witness (shades of Job's servants: "and I alone have escaped to tell thee . . .")?

What does it mean to witness an event which, when someone describes it, is not believable? What does it mean to witness an event which, when you inquire about it during your early years, no one hurries to describe?

What does it mean to witness an event which by your very survival, you negate?

The answer to these questions is that one experiences one's self as an utter fraud, and this sense of fraudulence carries its own apparatus of destructive corollaries. It is to experience the utter de-legitimization of one's childhood; it is to be penalized as no other child for the normal amnesia of pre-verbal childhood; it is to be discouraged into probing too deeply into one's past, out of fear that whatever is unearthed will by definition be illegitimate; it is to join the hapless roster of other self-invalidated witnesses – they for their madness, you for your infancy. It is to refuse to stand among fellow survivors who do remember, out of the conviction that you are not one of them. It is to smile stupidly at Holocaust memorial events, while they, when they can, weep.

It is also to piece one's life together on the basis of the accounts of others. Your story is never really your own, it is always what others tell you it is, you are dependent on *them* for your biography, and you can never let these authors go for fear that when they are gone, your story will be obliterated.

★

In 1992 I finally find the courage to go and look at this place called Bergen-Belsen. I cannot begin to describe the desperation I feel: let me find just one tree that is familiar, one barrack that will link *me* to that bleak past for which I suffer – so runs my prayers on the train ride into Germany. I arrive at the Memorial. There is a documentation center, and an historian appears at a desk.

"Can I help you?"

"I . . . I spent a couple of seasons here in summer camp. . . ." He does not smile. "Would you mind telling me your name?" he asks. He punches my name and my birth date into the computer. It begins to print furiously.

"You are on three lists, sir. One is the list of passengers on a train from Westerbork to Bergen-Belsen . . ." I cannot listen to the rest – he has said enough. The list says that I have indeed been there, it does what memory cannot do – my past was finally my own. It is okay not to like apples.

★

Oh, the dawn, the dawn.

Less than one thousand of The Hague's 35,000 Jews returned. The magnitude of this void, the initial realization of the enormity, of the scope of the murders, was more than the survivors could manage. No one had the coping mechanism for the synagogues that refused to fill, for the postwar return that didn't happen.

This was not about missing family and loved ones, it was about being the scattered remnants of something terrifying in its very vastness. It was a thunderclap from a slaughter larger than the human imagination.

In Bergen-Belsen, we slept dreamless like the dead. In The Hague, it was during the dawn that the nightmares first began – how we awakened screaming, how we sweated in our beds, our voices hoarse, dreading the night, dreading the enormous emptiness, dreading the camps we still inhabited. Thirty-four thousand inhabitants of The Hague (say it slowly) taken from our midst, taken while Humphrey Bogart and Ingrid Bergman played in the movies, taken when we already owned cars and radios. The trains and trolleys that took them away were still running.

In 2005, Rose, then well into her eighties, found me. She was one of the few who was a friend of my family before the war, and one of the few who survived, her husband with her.

"I became crazy after the war," Rose said, when I rushed to visit her in California. "It was impossible to be asleep or awake. I remember needing medication. It was all about the proportions of the tragedy, the vastness of it. And when we realized it, we could not live with it."

Rose's nightmares started to subside in the late 1950's; Mother's, as I recall, lasted longer.

What all this speaks to is the extraordinary unimportance of the year 1945. It marked the end of the war, but hardly the end of the Holocaust. The trauma of the Holocaust, only now being faced, only now being processed, hurtled through the 1950's and perhaps the 1960's. Survivors acted out; certainly many of the child survivors were next to impossible to parent, wild and unmanageable. And children born into these families – families for whom the Holocaust during these years was not a thing of the past but an ongoing reality – such children I would classify not as children of survivors, but as survivors themselves.

★

After the Holocaust, in 1946, the Jewish home for survivors in The Hague sold its leavening to a gentile before Passover, as Jews had been doing for thousands of years – it sold it as if the

Holocaust had never taken place. Not a beat was missed, not a hesitation apparent. I have in my possession the original certificate of sale. The Jews gathered at the table for this, my first *seder*, battered, limping, palsied, unreal, snuffling without joy, barely looking at each other. We sang *Dayenu* that year. That was the year I learned the melody.

They sang *Dayenu* that year – these Jews who in Westerbork had witnessed the hospital being emptied and its patients put on trains to Auschwitz thereby putting to bed any illusion that Auschwitz was a labor camp. These self-same Jews, who with the arrival of a new train every Tuesday morning heard the death knell toll for them. These Jews sang – If You had taken care of us in the wilderness, Almighty God, and not provided us with the manna – *Dayenu*, that would have been enough!

They sang *Dayenu* that year – these Jews who had their children snatched screaming from their hands in Westerbork and tossed onto the train to Sobibor, these self-same Jews who waved to their children as the train pulled out of the camp, a train no one in heaven nor upon the earth saw fit to stop, these Jews sang – If You had given us the manna, Almighty God, and had not given us the Holy Sabbath, *Dayenu*, that would have been enough!

They sang *Dayenu* that year – these Jews who had witnessed the departure of the last train to leave Westerbork for the east, the train filled with the *umbakante kinder*, the unknown children, the ones whose parents had preceded them on the train trips to the gasses and the shootings and the burnings, the children who had forgotten their names, who were inarticulate, who were pre-articulate, who held each other's hands, their eyes frozen in fear. These self-same Jews who screamed and never again slept through the night for having seen those eyes, these Jews sang – If You had given us the Holy Sabbath, Almighty God, and had not given us the Torah, *Dayenu*, that would have been enough.

They wept through *Dayenu* that year.

After the Holocaust.

CHAPTER NINE

Canada: "Plus ça change, plus c'est la même chose."

In 1948, I found the *Veendam* – the luxurious ocean liner on which we made the journey from Rotterdam to New York – nothing short of magnificent. It existed on a scale all its own. Never had I encountered anything of such proportions, of such magnitude – deck upon deck upon deck of endless grandeur. The ship's horns, sounding as we pulled out to sea, made me tremble.

★

Mother and I came up from our state room to watch Holland recede into the distance. I seem to remember the process happening too quickly.

We returned to the state room, where Mother became dreadfully seasick – a condition from which she had no respite for the full length of the voyage. She introduced me to French toast and tea, which I turn to even today at the slightest indication that

Passport picture of me, late 1948, for the journey to Canada.

I am getting sick, and which promptly brings me back to the luxurious *Veendam* and the round "Holland – America Lines" logo it favored everywhere.

Mother vomited endlessly, and it was only because she dealt with the lurching of the ship and the attendant heaving of her stomach with good humor, that I gave little thought to what was later to become my pit-deep anxiety – that not merely was she helpless, but that I too was helpless in the presence of her helplessness.

Soon the ship was mine. As in Bergen-Belsen, her infirmities brought me autonomy. There was nothing to keep me out of harm's way, yet somehow I never came to harm.

I did not open doors that were closed, I never got lost. I returned faithfully to our cabin to see how she was faring. As in Bergen-Belsen, she lay in bed and said wise things to me with great patience.

The *Veendam* stopped in Bermuda which I took in from its highest deck. I remember with perfect clarity how tiny the natives working on the docks appeared to me, and I hurried to Mother to tell her with great astonishment that here in Bermuda, people had black skin.

"Do they seem happy?" she asked.

"Yes," I replied, "they do."

"Mummy, may I go look some more?"

"Yes, Yozef, you may."

"Mummy," I asked, "if everybody is getting off the ship here, will we be alone with the captain when we go to New York?"

"People are just getting off to do a little shopping. Soon they will come back aboard and continue with us to New York."

"Mummy?"

"Yes, Yozef?"

"Mummy, why can't we also get off the ship and do shopping?"

"Because I am sick and very weak."

And there you have it. In subsequent years, for the most part, we never went anywhere, and few ever visited our home, save for a Saturday night pinochle game of old men. Mother's physical deformities and weakness, which she hated and which embarrassed her, ended up writing a script for my life – a life in which, like Mother, I became far more adept at imagining than at living – a script that has pursued me with some persistence since my Montreal days. But I am ahead of myself.

A day or two later we gather on the deck. Mother, her heaving stomach notwithstanding, does not want to miss Lady Liberty. The two ladies stare at each other. It was not their first encounter. She who sought to welcome the hungry, the poor, the wretched of the earth, did not manage to welcome us when we needed her;

not us and not six million others. Mother, without bitterness, without rancor, still believed in Lady Liberty's message, and somehow, today, sixty years after the retchingly glorious voyage of the *Veendam*, so do I.[1]

★

In the late 1920's, Grandmother, Grandfather and their six children moved from the Hague to Montreal, where grandfather took up as cantor of the Beth Yehudah Synagogue on Duluth Avenue. Grandfather, a St. Petersburg-trained tenor, was a star among stellar cantorial singers of his day. Josef Rosenblatt and other world-famous liturgy-artists often came to party and jam at his home, and there Mother accompanied all of them. Grandfather was known not just for his glorious voice and compositions, but also for his walks with his family on Fletcher's Field on Sabbath afternoons while wearing his white tuxedo. Grandfather eventually lost his shirt during the crash of Wall Street, and soon after, in 1935, died of a massive heart attack at the age of 49. Almost immediately after his death, Mother and her sister Rosie returned to Holland. To Mother, Canada meant nothing without her father, whom she had worshipped. In The Hague, Rosie suddenly contracted a fatal illness, and died unmarried. Mother met and married Father soon after she arrived in Holland. And that is how she was overtaken by the

1. Long after this chapter was written, I learned to my complete surprise that the Veendam had a remarkable history of squirreling Jews out of Holland during the early years of the Holocaust, mostly to safe ports in Europe and America. Its exploits are described in Bernard Wasserstein's extraordinary book on the fate of Dutch Jewry, *The Ambiguity of Virtue: Gertrude van Tijn and the Fate of the Dutch Jews*, London, Harvard University Press, 2014, pp. 82, 91.

*Mother and her mother in Montreal
at my Bar Mitzvah, October, 1955.*

Holocaust in Europe, while everyone else survived unscathed,
though poor, in Montreal.

★

And so it came to pass that at the end of December 1948 my
mother and I, on a train from the Port of New York to Montreal,
crossed the Canadian border at Rouse's Point, and made our
way to grandmother's apartment at 4485 A Esplanade Avenue.
There my mother's mother stared purposefully at her daughter,
took her in, gazed at a young woman whose hands were already
gnarled from rheumatic arthritis, whose legs were bent and stiff
and distended, who could not stand straight, and who walked
very poorly. So it came to pass that Grandmother looked over

her daughter and perceived in an instant the horrors that had befallen her. So it came to pass that mother said to daughter in quiet, certain terms, "I do not want ever to hear about what you went through in Europe. You are starting a new life here."

October 16th, 1942, was the day on which the ghetto in Piotrkow was liquidated. It was also the day I was born, elsewhere to the West.

Grandmother, on the other hand, *was* born in Piotrkow. I don't think she had the slightest idea of what transpired that day, although she always remembered my birthday.

In Piotrkow, in those autumnal days surrounding my birth, twenty thousand Jews were deported to Treblinka. I don't believe Grandmother ever knew what Treblinka was.

Uncle Jack had accompanied us on the train from New York to Montreal, where on the evening of this encounter between Grandmother and Mother, I was given a room with a balcony facing a courtyard which may have reminded Grandmother of Piotrkow.

My bed that evening was strewn with bright, beautiful toys. Not long before this encounter between Grandmother and Mother, attempts to rebuild the Jewish community of Piotrkow were halted when several Jews returning there were murdered as they tried to reclaim their houses.[2]

Was it possible to reclaim your life after the Holocaust? Was it possible, for that matter, to go on? The Poles told the returning Jews, No, you no longer exist. Grandmother, albeit less violently, but with no less drama, said the same to Mother.

And I, oblivious to all these disconnects, did not have the

2. *Encyclopedia of the Holocaust*, vol. 3, p. 1135. My language here is almost a full quote from this article.

Uncle Jack, in the late 1940's, following his discharge from the US Army. Mother related that he saved our lives more than once when she informed several nervous and gullible SS personnel that her brother Jack was in the US Army "looking for us." He never made it overseas but spent most of his military career washing army dishes in New York and New Jersey. When I turned 14 he took me to my first movie in a theater: the Belmont Theater on Mt. Royal Avenue in Montreal. It was called "Woman's Prison" and starred Ida Lupino.

faintest idea of what to do with all these toys, not even how to play with them.

Perhaps, had I been somewhat older, I might have sat on the bed and said, "Now then, God, now that Hitler is dead and the war is ended, would You like to resume our conversation?

"We can no longer meet in History, God, too much has transpired. We can't seem to find You there, You don't seem to be in any of the old places. Where shall we meet, God?"

And He might have answered, "In Creation, which is unaffected by History. And in the texts of the Torah, which weep with deep longing for their murdered Jews." Had He thus replied, I would have been disappointed. I would have wanted to meet Him in Piotrkow.

Uncle Jack, who was neither religious nor married, and who had taken us to Macy's only yesterday, came in to put me to bed. No man had ever done that for me before.

★

Reverend Roness was a short, firm, handsome man with a moustache, silver-framed glasses, and a cleft chin. He arrived in our apartment calmly one evening to teach me – age 6, to read Hebrew.

Several such evenings took place. Grandmother let him in – he removed his coat, then his fedora, he put on an elegant black kippah, sat down at the kitchen table and the lesson would begin.

The Hebrew alphabet is simple to learn, as are its separate vowels, and I mastered it in no time in the early Montreal winter evenings, in the warmth of the apartment with its blond furniture and hard sofas, and in the calm warmth of my teacher's kindness. He was strictly business as he assumed what is by far Judaism's most sacred ministry – extending the tradition to the next generation.

But my learning was destined to be different from all other learning. When children are finally ready to put consonant and vowel together to read, then what is normally chosen for them is the Shema, the quiet acceptance of God's unity and our submission to and vulnerability before His grandeur and omniscience.

The curriculum for me was different. The thrill of finally being able to read those beautiful letters was served on a cold tray of morbidity – *Yisgadal v'yiskadash*, I read. "You need to recite the prayer for the dead," they said to me, "for your father."

And they were in a hurry. I was dispatched alone at dawn to the synagogue around the corner, where I found myself in a row of mourners reciting Kaddish swaying slowly in a faithful rhythm. Men in their fifties and sixties, working class, Yiddish-speaking, grief-stricken for their departed loved ones. I stood among them and did my duty for my ghostly father whom I did not remember and did not love, and whom I wished was here to guide me.

Reverend Roness stopped coming.

The Kaddish reciters had something about them. The synagogue saves the mourner's Kaddish for the end of the service, at which time the mourners come from all points of the sanctuary and stand facing the Ark, firmly and resolutely accepting God's Kingship and Providence – the finality of His decisions about who shall live and who shall die. These particular tired European immigrants, mostly Polish, many survivors, didn't walk to the front, they shuffled and dragged their feet, they wore old creaky shoes from Opatow and Chestachova, from Chelm and from Lodz, their feet raised the dreary dust of endless Jewish wandering. As they came together from all ends of the sanctuary, they frightened me with their unpressed suit pants and their weary bulks. I heard thunder in their gait and as I gathered in between them each morning – barely reaching their waists, intimidated by the din, calmed by no one – I felt shame at having been to a kingdom no one would talk about. Three years later, I continued to have an embarrassing deathly pallor which mother explained came from the worst case of jaundice in all of Bergen-Belsen, a pallor so alarming that I was constantly stared at, and yet never questioned about. I was also deeply ashamed of occasionally having to sit with mother in the synagogue in the upstairs women's balcony, and again, unlike the other kids, of having no father.

★

This synagogue had a cantor and choir. I, who stemmed from a glorious cantorial family, I who had perfect pitch, and a voice that was a gift, auditioned for the choir, and failed the audition as later, when I read Torah in the Junior Congregation, I experienced a terrible singing problem: the words came out far faster than they should have – "You must stop swallowing your words," they said to me, "you must slow down."

An old man who loved being with the kids took me aside. He had a white moustache, beautifully trimmed, and was a monument maker by trade. He disclosed that he, as a child, had had the same problem. He had stammered, he confided in me, he had swallowed his words, and he had been unpleasant to listen to. "But I fixed it," he said, "I fixed it by disciplining myself like steel to simply control my lips and to sing it and to say it at a pace slow enough so that it came out just as I wanted it."

He was right, and eventually it worked. I didn't know that other child survivors also suffered from this problem – language after the Holocaust is inadequate for what's inside you. You become unusually quiet, singing is next to impossible, and when they do jump out, words seem to come from someone else and some other place. I forgot my Dutch almost entirely in what seemed to be a matter of weeks, and my English, which also settled in no time, was accent-free. Yiddish was Grandmother's spoken tongue; that language too swiftly and effortlessly became entirely intuitive. I had much language, nothing I could say, no father, and a past that seemed to me to be filled with mud.

★

The courtyard we lived in, the one that must have reminded Grandmother of Piotrkow, was European both in its architecture and in its demography. Many of the families that lived here were Yiddish-speaking, several of them survivors.

As the endless Montreal ice-sharp winter melted into balmy spring evenings, dozens of kids would huddle bareheaded on the stairs at the end of the long walkway that led from the courtyard to the street, where they sang "Heart of My Heart" and where they overlooked the massive rectangles of grass, blocks long. That was the playground of Fletcher's Field, complete with esplanades and benches, baseball diamonds, and soccer fields. Just beyond, across Park Avenue (pronounced, at the time, as "Par Kavenue") lay Mt. Royal.

The mountain never failed to startle with its mega-presence – a mountain you could ski down in the heart of a city, crowned with a three-hundred foot-high crucifix. During these balmy spring evenings, as night descended with great tranquility, the magisterial crucifix would light up with thousands of bulbs, and in its overbearing way, frightened me.

I was too young to understand the connection of the cross to Father's murder, but understood that this cross, which, with the flick of a switch, effortlessly overwhelmed the night silhouette of the whole city, had a message. I experienced it with great misgiving, if not outright terror.

Some twenty kids, from my age to young teens, were sitting on these concrete stairs enjoying the languorous evenings. The group included the two daughters of the H. family, all-Canadian, which while Jewish, was anomalously English-speaking. Because of this, to us children, they were aristocracy.

No parent in the courtyard ever spoke to me, save for Mr. H., who parked his red Ford pickup (with "H. Plumbing" emblazed on both of its doors) every evening at six o'clock in front of the courtyard entrance where we children sat. There was ritual here: Each day he would step down heavily from his vehicle which was filled with endless arrangements of pipes, valves, elbows, and rods, cross the sidewalk, pass around the children, and after first kissing his girls, would greet me:

"Hi Joseph, how are you? How is your mother?"

He addressed all of my being. He was present without being intrusive. He engaged me with respect and compassion. He had a round face, glasses as I recall, and a perpetual heavy six o'clock shadow framed by a carefully-tended moustache. His face had folds and ridges that I thought made him handsome. I even liked the smell of the pipe-fitting grease he exuded. The older of his two girls was my age (six or seven) and adopted a motherly attitude towards me.

One day Mr. H. came out of the truck very slowly. The beard stubble looked heavier, the folds and ridges of his face had drawn inward in deep, craggy crevices, sharp and forbidding. The fatigue he exuded was unbearable.

The next morning he was dead. A massive heart attack, the kids said.

Fathers.[3]

★

Something came up for me recently while watching the 1985 TV-film, *Hitler's SS: Portrait of Evil* (directed by Jim Goddard,

---

3. After writing these lines, I finally found one of the sisters living in Atlanta. "How accurate is my memory?" I asked her, after I had read the relevant lines to her. "Terrific," she replied, "except that Dad died of cancer." In this particular case, I wondered whether history is better served by memory than by truth. I decided that both had their place.

and starring, among others, Jose Ferrer and Tony Randal). The
SS officer, processing Jews and arranging for their liquidation,
encounters in the pitiful line-up before him an elderly man
(played by Ferrer), whom he recognizes to be one of his brother's
revered professors. Without batting an eyelash, with shrewdness
and wit, he pulls him aside and saves him from certain doom. The
professor, incredulous, manages monosyllables, says nothing –
there is clearly too much to say.

What came up for me here was something about a soldier,
in this case trained to accomplish the unspeakable, still able to
perform, deep in the heart of evil, an act at once sane and kind.
I knew also, that I had seen this before, in life and not just in the
movies; indeed, that I too had benefitted from such largesse (if
that is the word).

I feel as though I too had met such a person while I was still
a toddler. No clear memory, but the very deep feeling of male
kindness emerging from this scene overwhelmed me. Perhaps it
was the SS officer in Bergen-Belsen who made me into his mascot, who made me into his atonement. Perhaps it was the U.S.
serviceman from the African-American motorized unit with
his reassuring, amazingly polished boots, who in the rain drove
me and several other surviving Jewish ruffians – wild, hungry,
orphaned and stateless – to the train station in Leipzig for the
journey home.

This mysterious persona, together with his act of deep male
kindness, rests, waiting, inside me; he inhabits me. Is it he who
caused me to be attracted to the rabbinate, certainly to its pastoral
side? His feeling of caregiving sits within me; persists to this day.

Indeed, it is to him that I revert when someone shattered by
illness, loss or human failure comes to me. And when I try to
console and rebuild, it is his image that inspires me, that provides

me with a composure I act out when needed, of comfort and wisdom.

He was inside me even before I became a rabbi. I was in the third grade of the Bancroft School in Montreal (Mrs. Lieberman's class – we are talking academic year 1950–51) wearing hand-me-down Fleet Foot sneakers, which I thought tremendously cool (a word no one would have used at the time), and finding myself in the class play. I remember nothing about the play; not the title, not the content, not the plot. I played the father. My classmate Rhoda, at Mrs. Lieberman's request, brought me the prop: her father's pipe. Miracle of miracles, I, without father, without even stepfather at that point, knew how to present myself credibly to the audience as soon as the pipe bit hit my teeth. I knew how to be wise, I knew how to be kind, I knew how to be authoritative. I did the part without difficulty; I knew as Martin Heidegger, Hannah Arendt and Martin Buber were all saying at the time, how to be.

★

Circa 1954, Mother remarried. For me, she always said, so I would have a father. Nice guy, too.

I wasn't invited to the wedding. I was too sallow, too pale, too volatile, too unpredictable. I reminded whoever saw me of hunger, disease, and death. I didn't have a place at joyous occasions. I saw bride and groom drive off in the blue Plymouth, dressed to kill and happy, with nary a thought of what all this might mean to me.

My hostess, Mrs. G., was close to 90, filled with love and very attentive. She even provided me with reading materials: I read love comics that whole night – I don't know that I slept at all. Couples falling for each other, endless kissing. I totally didn't get it. Come to think of it, I don't think anyone had kissed me by then, unless Grandmother's occasional slobbering on my cheek counted.

After the marriage there was a new family to meet: his. They had summer homes in a Laurentian village by the name of Prefontaine, and pretended, up to a point, that I was one of them.

Prefontaine was known for its exquisite clean air and tuberculosis sanatorium, which terrified me to the point where I didn't want to breathe outside, lest I catch some of the dreaded microbes. Prefontaine had a lovely rolling river where people fished and swam, a synagogue, a ritualarium, and a pool hall where they sold pink ice cream called tootsie-pootsie, and where teenagers gathered for hours to flirt endlessly. I never swam, I never fished, I never flirted, and it would not be much of an exaggeration to say that I never spoke. "You're so quiet, Joseph," I was told repeatedly. I never replied.

The year Mother married, an iceman came every few days to the Prefontaine cottages to deliver a new, massive block for the icebox. The house also got fitted with a new indoor toilet. Once it was installed, Mother and I were told rather unceremoniously that the new toilet was only for veteran members of the immediate family, but that she and I were welcome to use the old outhouse that was still happily ensconced some thirty yards down the path leading to the railroad tracks.

To my horror, at this announcement Mother was immediately transported to the excremental assault that was Bergen-Belsen. I could feel the feces on the straw mattresses attacking her nostrils again, I could hear her retching just thinking about the communal outhouse toilets, where there never were enough seats and where the people with diarrhea (half the camp) couldn't wait. Although she didn't say it, I knew she was thinking that where you shit *is* important, and even more important, therefore, is who *decides* where you shit. She would have none of it. "My legs," she said, "are not flexible enough to travel this path and fight the weeds and the grass." That night she screamed at her new husband for not speaking up in outrage, and later, wept quietly. Having a father, I reflected, might turn out to be costly.

I, on the other hand, loved the outhouse and frequented it all the time. There was something familiar, even comforting about it; perhaps it provided me with a badly-needed dose of my past.

★

Sixty years later, I learned that in my third grade Montreal class, fully a third of my fellow pupils were child survivors. Needless to say, the topic never came up. I was also informed that my deathly pallor pursued me to my Bar Mitzvah, but that is beyond where this telling ends.

CHAPTER TEN

The Last Witness:
Who is left to remember the Holocaust?

Imagine it: the end of an era. The last person able to testify to all that transpired, to all that befell us, the last person who could affirm that we indeed saw what we saw, is gone. Of all the rememberers, I alone am left to sit here, knowing that my time will also come. And then, what becomes of the tale?

I am limited in what I remember; I was not yet three when the war ended. What value is there in the few horrific scenes I can conjure? The historical record is not enriched by them. My memory has become a datum, a relic. Valid, but inessential.

While they still lived, I stood among the other survivors, seasoned, wizened men and women who were perpetually old, prematurely gaunt. Their bodies reflected those days. The deep shadows of what they had once taken in never left them.

They would glance at me in passing, surveying my inconsequentiality, often with patience, often without. I was a fly. "Do you really know, child," they would ask, "do you really know what it is to have your parents shot before your eyes, do you really know what it is to have your grandparents thrown out of the upstairs window during a liquidation?"

Did I know? I would put my hands in my pockets and shrug, looking, in those early days, for a cigarette. Did I know? The question was an accusation. You do not understand, they were saying, you were too young to make sense of it. The carnage and death, the murder by fever and by hunger – all of which I witnessed, some of which I experienced – were not valid to them because I could not have made sense of such experiences as they occurred. My testimony was that of a blind man. I heard the noises, put it all together later; not acceptable in a court of law, not sufficiently real.

"You say you were there," they argued. "But you really weren't."

Then they would appear astonished at the pain that came over my face from such invalidation and would hastily take pity.

"*Bist geven a yingeleh*," they would say. It's not your fault, you were just a kid. Children, they meant, are frivolous; let's not take their experiences seriously.

They are all gone now. Their hoary heads and Polish teeth have crossed the great divide, and I alone, I alone am left to tell the tale. I'm a bit of a fake, don't you think? A bit of a liar, no?

When those memories I did possess would beckon, I trembled. Sleepless nights would become my lot, filled with chills and despair. They were without solace, without consolation. I would not allow love. Love promised that what little memory I did have would be submerged. Love meant the cesspool that was Bergen-Belsen would disappear.

When I was 10 years old, my father murdered, my mother married a man in Montreal who forbade mention of the

Holocaust. Shall we let it disappear, I wondered? And if we did, would I continue being? I lived with him but did not take up with him.

I did not, could not, remember what brought on my nocturnal fits of madness; there were no visual scenes in my imagination when primordial terrors wracked my body. I could not remember why I would periodically get mammoth rheumatic tremors that seized me in the darkness and in the light. I did not remember why Mother's moans of terror shuddered within me decades after she died. I knew that I was afraid of her, not for what she had been but for what she had become. I knew that I did not have, did not want to have, the toughness in her that allowed her to survive. Yet did it enter me, yet does it overtake me. It turns people away when they sense it; I am not easy to love.

For all that, I did not visit my past, really, never gave it a glance, until I turned 50. Slowly I stared at it, slowly, with index cards, I put it in chronological order: the Hague, Westerbork, Bergen-Belsen, the Hague.

Soon after the end of the Holocaust, in Montreal, I fell in with other child survivors. They made up fully a third of my seventh-grade class. We were silent about our past. When the topic came up, we would become restless and look about anxiously for distraction. We did not want to be witnesses; we just wanted to be like everyone else. Eventually we each became an anti-witness. We didn't want to hear about it, talk about it; we pretended that the ordeal happened to others, to those who did have numbers on their arms. Perhaps we understood that the mature survivors constituted the most humiliated group of people on earth, and we wanted no part of their residual shame.

Mother died when I turned 40. Freddie, a tad older than I, came to sit with me at her shivah.

"Do you remember, Joseph," he said, "do you remember how

we used to play hide-and-seek around the corpses in Bergen-Belsen?"

I did not remember, but it was this question, coming from him, that allowed me to accept myself as a survivor. And it has taken nearly three decades following that shivah for me to have learned that what my mind does not remember, my body does, and so does my soul.

Hesitantly I take my place among the survivors. I get into the line at the gates of the death camps, and I am there, more in death than in life.

And so I sometimes entertain this fantasy that, because of my sheer youth during those years, I am the Last Witness. The Holocaust will pass out of experience and into history. There will be no one left to say "and then they took my parents away and I never saw them again," or "Moishalleh died in my arms; he had not eaten anything in two weeks and his nine-year-old frame could not take it any more," or "my high school teacher examined all the boys in the class, and all the circumcised ones were expelled."

I carry this fear that when I disappear, so will the last memories of that great darkness, so will the fecal stench that attended the typhus, so will the ravages of the outdoors that attended the roll calls, and the stiffness, everywhere, of the corpses. And in the absence of such primary memories, how long will it take for a civilized country again to allow a leader into office who harbors evil beliefs and insidious desires? And how long until the physicians and lawyers and judges and philosophers and writers and musicians and composers and conductors join his cause?

I wonder: If I indeed turn out to be the Last Witness, will my death mark the beginning of the Great Forgetting?

At such moments, fortunately, I have also come to realize

the arrogance of such questions, and to understand that such arrogance is where idolatry and atheism begin.

For I will not be the Last Witness; the Last Witness will be the greatest, the most humiliated Witness of all. I speak of course, of God Himself. He Who is everywhere had to have been there, too. He had to have been present, and He had to have witnessed His reputation as redeemer and savior of Israel sink into the mud of Treblinka and Belzec.

"What will the Egyptians say?" Moses asks when God threatens to destroy Israel after they worship the Golden Calf. "Do you want them to say that You took the Jews out of Egypt only so that You might destroy them Yourself when they reached the desert?"

The argument worked; He was averse to being misconstrued.

There is a scene in the great Rolf Hochhuth play The Deputy in which a priest asks the character Hochhuth, based on Josef Mengele, something along the line of, "Have you no fear of divine retribution? Do you not believe that God will call you to account for this?"

And Mengele is made to answer: "You have no idea, no idea, how I wish with all my heart that He strike me down, that He slay me every time I send a child to the gas. But He doesn't."

No one came out of the Holocaust looking worse than God. He is compassionate, the theologians used to say! He hates evil, they claimed! Omnipotent, they said! Caring for His chosen people, the liturgy reads: "*Ha-oneh le'amo yisrael be-et shavom elav*" ("He Who answers the prayer of His people whenever they turn to Him"). Not this time, not six million times.

Yet although He did not save six million of His people, in an extraordinary reversal of roles and of history, His people, the ones who did survive, saved Him.

The rabbis who escaped the infernos spent scant time contemplating, much less bemoaning what the philosopher Martin Buber has called the eclipse of God.

"With ten trials was Abraham tested," the Mishnah recalls, and he passed them all. Why didn't Abraham ask God all those moral questions about his final trial, the binding of Isaac? "Didn't you just promise me a chapter ago that my seed will come through Isaac? What am I now supposed to tell people about divine commitments? Is Isaac guilty of something that merits the death penalty? With respect to Isaac, shall the Judge of all the earth not do justice?" Abraham, who clearly knows such questions, does not ask them. When you are in love, as Abraham was with God, your love sabotages all such inquiries. Rashi, the great medieval teacher and exegete, says it most clearly: *Lo hirher ahar midotav merov ahavato* ("Because of his great love for God, Abraham was not interested in God's intentions and agendas").

The rabbi of Zanz-Klausenberg, who came out of the camps shaven and shrunk, raged for years about his Holocaust experiences, yet skipped nary a beat in his loving worship of his creator, and embarked almost at once on a successful campaign to build a hospital. The rabbis of Bobov, Ungvar, and Satmar created housing for the poor and provided food programs for the infirm. Like the rabbi of Modzhits, another survivor, who composed and sang his way through the 1950s and 1960s, they built houses of worship, ritual baths, and educational institutions in numbers unmatched ever in Jewish history.

The mighty theological questions emerging from that muddy darkness, they found, merely led back to the gates of Auschwitz, and they chose not to go back there. Never would they be humiliated again, and never again would they permit God such humiliation.

And they had confidence that He Who commands the dawn to follow the night will represent them fairly when the last witness is gone, that He Himself will report on the heroism of the victims and on how, in their last moments, they sanctified His name.

The Last Witness will join the legions of victims in the celestial palace that is touted as the place where Elijah, in God's presence, will provide the mighty answers –including one that deals with the great absence while one-and-a-half million Jewish children were being murdered.

Two lines will form in Heaven, each of them silent. No one will be *asking* Elijah a thing.

The first line, with Dostoevsky as its guide, might say: "Elijah, tell God that we really have no interest in post-facto explanations about His great absence; it's just too late for explanations, too much injustice, too much cruelty has been allowed to happen. The notion of an adequate answer to such horror is itself repulsive."

The second line, forming the dialectic, would have Abraham as its guide. It might assert, "It was never about us, Elijah; we never sought, and still don't need, explanations. It was always about God. We just couldn't bear His vast humiliation, and we did what we could to mitigate it. Blessed be His name for ever and ever."

And, were I the Last Witness, I would rage against both camps and ask how dare they remain silent, what self-absorbed luxury were they indulging, anyway, when the memory of that time, of those children, is in danger of dissipating?

"Where is God?" I would thunder at Elijah. "Is He out there reciting the names of the camps? Belsen, Treblinka, Majdanek, Sobibor? Is He reading the names of the victims?" I would pound the tables with both hands. "Is He weeping?"

Epilogue

My story then – certainly as much of it as I wanted to write – is over.

Yet one of my editors said, "You can't leave the story there. Your readers know who you are, who you've become, what you've made of your life. Leave them, at the very least, with a few more details."

Here they are:

I don't think I ever grew up. Almost to the present, I find myself fully comfortable only among young people, not adults, not even adults younger than me. I'm often astonished to find that I am older than some of the grown-ups who continue to frighten me with their social comforts and certainties.

The horrors that accompanied my toddler years, which continue to play hide-and-seek, now appearing, now self-denying, in their noir brevity, cry out for affirmation, for authentication, for validation. Yet for the longest time, all I had to go on was first my pallor and later, what I can only call my existential vacuity, by which I mean my incapacity to believe that who I am is serious, what I do is serious, what I write is serious.

So profoundly did I disbelieve my Holocaust past that I eventually began to doubt my birth, and I began to experience myself as a stray, wanted by no one and of no interest to anyone. The early years in Montreal, although not without fun, not without friends, achieved some legitimacy in my heart and spirit as long as no reference was made to the camps, or to my father.

Mother married a decent, well-intentioned man in 1953, who when I was brought along to the new Outremont apartment, did not bargain for my rebelliousness, for my Holocaust madness, did not understand why, when he told me to take on his surname and drop my father's, I bit him and ran out of the house.

He didn't understand why I did this, especially since I didn't remember my father. To this day I don't understand it either.

Although in my stepfather's will he referred to me as his beloved son, it rang false and seemed to echo a law manual with boilerplate forms. He never adopted me. When he tried to punish me, always appropriately, he learned that I would hit him back in what I intended as self-defense towards a stranger.

"You're not my father," I would say to him on such occasions, as if it was his fault. He would look back at me as if to say, "You can say that again."

He left me great gifts – my love of the Sabbath and synagogues among them. When Mother died, he wept and said his Queen was gone. She was, but I didn't weep because, I thought then, it takes a grown-up to weep.

I attended the local yeshiva, administered and taught by Yiddish-speaking escapees of Poland during the first years of the Holocaust – men who had nothing but limitless love for and patience with me, and nothing but respect for Mother, who they understood to be a heroine, and of whom they were somewhat afraid.

As a result, I became in those days, and remain in many ways still, a Polish Jew in a time-warp, my Dutch origins becoming a source of enormous discomfort and disaffection.

I became a regular disciple of the Chief Rabbi, who would admit no disciples. When twice a year, he lectured at the synagogue filled with an awe-struck audience of several hundred, we may as well have been in Piotrkow – the language, the Torah-based Yiddish, the darkening chapel, the hushed, bearded faces, not to mention the sacred subject matter, and notwithstanding the Fords and Chevy's and Studebakers whizzing by outside on St. Urbain Street, we – the people, the scene, were utterly interchangeable with the best that Jewish Poland had to offer only fifteen years earlier. Thus did the Dutch Jewish boy from post-Depression The Hague metamorphose into a seamlessly authentic Polish yeshiva student.

I attended university where I studied psychology, read the Romantic Poets and Melville, Descartes and Kant, Nietzsche and Trilling, and where I also read Penguin classics without number, and often without regard to title. I rejected a career in opera and became instead a rabbi with a bent for performance.

I married and divorced because no one could live with me. I married again, and it has lasted for over thirty years. From both marriages I have five children, eleven grandchildren, and everyone among the sundry offspring seems to like each other. I still sing, though mostly in the shower.

For over forty years I have been a university chaplain whereby my love of Torah, which brings me endless consolation and inspiration, is able to continue its provocative dance with students and faculty. Yet I remain at heart a Dutch castaway who has evaded all memory of Westerbork and Bergen-Belsen, and who is happiest pretending to be a Polish, pre-Holocaust Jew, a survivor of I-know-not-what, but ultimately of the European darkness that still blankets history and memory with its horrors, and as I have said earlier, just won't go away.

Acknowledgements

Elie Wiesel, at most of our weekly Torah study sessions at Boston University, unrelentingly encouraged this book from when I first thought of writing it.

Commentary magazine, under its previous editor, Neal Kozodoy, firmly believed in me as a writer. Two of the chapters, "The Lost Transport," and "The Last Survivor" first appeared in its pages (the latter under the editorship of Jon Podhoretz), and I am grateful for their permission to reprint these chapters unchanged in this book.

Renata Adler, Alan Rosen, Blu Greenberg, Robert Krell, Vivien Markow-Speiser and Lilka Elbaum, each in his/her own time and way, took on the roles of coach and/or editor, and urged me on.

The late great editor-in-chief of Random House, Sam Vaughan, believed in this book even more than I did, and the manuscript benefited enormously from his suggestions, as it did later on from the efforts and edits of the poets and writers Merle Feld and Dale Norman. Rabbi Michael Swirsky was the first audience for the chapter entitled "Tanya," in all its post-partum fragility, and the gravity of his attending to my reading of it still resonates with me.

When I needed to finally face my Holocaust history and bring it to some coherence, Yaakov Walters was completely there for me. He helped me find Shlomo Samson, who not only was the head of the burial society that paid last respects to the prisoners who died during the Lost Transport, but who sat with me far more recently in Tel Aviv with an extraordinarily military overlay map and helped bring my story into coherence. Michael Schneeberger of Kitzingen, Germany, did the same for me even earlier, and thereby helped made this book possible.

Shlomo Abrahams, Adon Menat, David Gilai, Frank Epstein, Chaja Verveer, Manfred Pfeiffer, and Dr. Elisheva Van der Hal allowed me to interview them. Picking their prodigious brains and memories did wonders to improve my understanding of the Shoah, and provided the constant moral support the writing needed.

Dr. Bart van der Boom helped me traverse the arcane bowels of NIAD, the Dutch War historical society in Amsterdam, and the late Is Van Creveld, author of seven books on the history of the Jews in The Hague, gave unstintingly of his time and showed me sides of my family history that I would never have otherwise found. Jack Boas was sympathetic and helpful discussing Westerbork, and Rose de Lieme and her sons opened their hearts and archives to me.

Tim Hays worked tirelessly to bring this book to public attention, Geoffrey Norman gave it the legal attention it needed, while Jonathan Cohen was far more patient with photographs than I could ever have been.

My family read the chapters as they were born. Aaron and Karyn, Rivka, Yankel, Ilonka and Aharon, Zissie and Brian — they and their kids, brought light to the intense darkness that encounters with the Holocaust bring, and made me a proud parent and grandparent.

Boston University, its administrations and faculty, and the boards, alumni and students of its Florence and Chafetz Hillel House gave me a context and love that few authors have been privileged to experience.

My wife Reizel is my best reader and friend. What Akiva, perhaps the greatest rabbinic sage of antiquity, said about his Rachel, I say about Reizel:

> all that is mine,
> all that is theirs,
> is utterly yours.

And above all, the Almighty Himself, never far from my side, together with His great Torah, inspire me each day, making me humble and grateful.

JOSEPH POLAK is an infant survivor of the Holocaust, during which time he was a prisoner at two concentration camps: Westerbork and Bergen-Belsen. He has published extensively in leading popular and scholarly periodicals and newspapers, including the *Boston Globe*, *Commentary*, *Jewish Law Studies*, *Judaism*, and *Tradition*. He is an assistant professor of public health (health law) at the Boston University School of Public Health; the rabbi emeritus of the Florence and Chafetz Hillel House at Boston University; and the chief justice at the Rabbinical Court of Massachusetts. He lives in Brookline, Massachusetts.

ELIE WIESEL is a Romanian-born Holocaust survivor, author of 57 books, and winner of the 1986 Nobel Peace Prize. He lives in New York.